# PUBLIC SPEAKING STUDENT WORKBOOK

Karen Kangas Dwyer, Ph.D.

# PUBLIC SPEAKING STUDENT WORKBOOK

*PUBLIC SPEAKING STUDENT WORKBOOK, Edition 2021*

Copyright @ Karen Kangas Dwyer, PhD
Editions: 1996, 2010…2020

ISBN: 978-1-7334218-7-4

All rights reserved. No part of this book may be reproduced or stored in a retrieval system in any form whatsoever, by photography or xerography, by broadcast or transmission or by any other electronic means, by translation into any kind of language, or otherwise, without written permission from the author, except by a reviewer, who may quote brief passages in critical articles or reviews.

Printed in the United States of America

## *INTRODUCTION*

Welcome to the Public Speaking Course! This course is designed to help you develop lifetime skills for communicating with others in a public or large group setting. These important skills will improve your personal confidence and competence and will ultimately help you in your academic, social, and professional life.

As public speaking instructors, we know that you may be enrolled in this class only because it fulfills the university's general education requirement for a public speaking course. We also know that you may have a lot of apprehension about public speaking and this class. However, we encourage you to approach this course with an openness and willingness to learn. Together, we can transform your apprehension into positive and empowering experiences of personal growth. In fact, you may be pleasantly surprised at how much you will enjoy this class and how useful this course will prove to be in helping you attain your future goals.

## **ASSIGNMENTS AND EXERCISES**

This *Public Speaking Student Workbook* is designed to accompany your public speaking textbook and to provide you with important information regarding course policies and the required speeches. In addition, this workbook includes many of your classroom assignments and exercises, as well as helpful exam review guides. Please plan to bring this workbook to each class session.

Public Speaking Student Workbook
*TABLE OF CONTENTS*

**INTRODUCTION, iii**

**CHAPTER ONE: COURSE POLICIES AND STUDENT INFORMATION**
Course Policies, Goals, & Student Responsibilities, 2-4
Professional Classroom Etiquette and Netiquette, 5
Academic Integrity, 6
Criteria for Evaluating Speeches, 7-8
Student Information Sheet, 9
Myself as a Communicator Paper, 10

**CHAPTER TWO: MANAGING COMMUNICATION APPREHENSION**
Conquering Speech Anxiety Journal Assignment, 12
Managing Fear, Nervousness, and Anxiety, 13
Assessing Your Communication Apprehension Level, 14
Scoring and Interpreting Your Scores, 15-16
The Cognitive Restructuring Technique, 17-20
Discovering and Disengaging Anxious Thoughts, 17
Unproductive Thoughts List, 18
Positive Coping Statements, 19
The Formula for Building Confidence, 20
Diaphragmatic Breathing for Reducing Anxiety, 21

**CHAPTER THREE: GETTING STARTED**
My Persona Mini-Speech, 25
Instructor Feedback Form & Checklist for Mini-Speech Option #1, 26
The Colleague Introduction Mini-Speech, 27
Instructor Feedback Form & Checklist for Mini-Speech Option #2, 28
The Leisure Time and Visual Aid Mini-Speech, 29
Instructor Feedback Form & Checklist for the Leisure Time Mini-Speech, 30
Topic Selection Exercise, 31
Possible Topics for Informative Speeches, 32
Specific Purpose and Central Idea Guidelines, 33-34
Specific Purpose and Central Idea Exercise, 35-36
Informative Group Mini-Speech Assignment & Feedback form, 37-38
Informative Group Mini-Speech Outline, 39
Mind-Mapping Assignment, 40
Organizational Patterns Assignment, 41
Ten Rules for Outlining, 42-43
Example of Formal Preparation Outline Format, 44
Example of Delivery Outline - 5" x 8" Speaker's Card, 45
Citing Your Sources and Making Your References, 46
Speech Introduction Exercise, 47
Introducing the Speaker, 48
Introducing the Speaker Worksheet, 49

**CHAPTER FOUR: INFORMATIVE SPEAKING**

Informative Speech Assignment #1—Process Speech,  51-52
Topic, Specific Purpose, and Central Idea Report #1,  53
Presentational Slides Assignment and Guidelines,  54
Instructor Evaluation Form for Informative Speech #1,  55
Informative Speech #1—Speaker Checklist,  56
Self-Evaluation Form for Informative Speech #1,  57-58
In-class Audience Analysis Questionnaire Activity,  59
Sample Audience Analysis Survey,  60
Analyzing Supporting Material,  61
Informative Speech #2—Speaker Checklist,  62
Informative Speech Assignment #2 and Library Assignment,  63-64
Topic, Specific Purpose, Central Idea and Research Report #2,  65
Information Literacy: Researching and Citing Sources,  66
Citing Sources Assignment,  67-68
Instructor Evaluation Form for Informative Speech #2,  69
My Audience Analysis Summary for Informative Speech #2,  70
Self-Evaluation Form for Informative Speech #2,  71-72
Using Vivid Language Assignment,  73
Formal Preparation Outline Peer Review Activity,  74

## CHAPTER FIVE: PERSUASIVE SPEAKING
Basic Persuasive Theory and Concepts,  76-77
Coactive Strategies and Refutation Organizational Pattern,  78
Motivated Sequence Mini-Speech,  79
Instructor Feedback Form for Motivated Sequence Mini-Speech,  80
Topics for Persuasive Speeches Worksheet,  81
Fact, Value, Policy Assignment,  82
Persuasive Dyad Speech #1—Speaker Checklist,  83
Example of Dyad Persuasive Speech Outline,  84
Motivated Sequence Group Speech Outline,  85
Possible Topics for Persuasive Speeches,  86
Persuasive Dyad Speech Assignment #1—Non-profit,  87
Persuasive Dyad Speech Contract,  88
Persuasive Speech Assignment #1—Individual,  89-90
Monroe's Motivated Sequence Outline Format,  91
Motivated Sequence Steps Chart,  92
Topic, Specific Purpose, Central Idea, and Research Report, Persuasion #1,  93
Citing Sources Assignment---Persuasive Speech #1,  94
Instructor Evaluation Form for Persuasive Dyad Speech #1,  95
Self-Evaluation Form for Persuasive Speech #1,  97-98
Persuasive Speech Assignment #2,  99-100
Topic, Specific Purpose and Central Idea Persuasion #2,  101
Citing Sources Assignment---Persuasive Speech #2  102
Instructor Evaluation Form for Persuasive Speech #2,  103
My Audience Analysis Summary for Persuasive Speech #2,  104

Persuasive Speech #2—Speaker Checklist, 105
Self-Evaluation Form for Persuasive Speech #2, 107-108

## CHAPTER SIX: CEREMONIAL SPEAKING
Ceremonial Speaking Assignment, 110
Specific Guidelines for Ceremonial Speeches, 111-113
Commemorative Speech Planning Worksheet, 114
Organization for Commemorative Speeches, 115
Topic, Specific Purpose, and Central Idea Report for the Ceremonial Speech, 117
Commemorative Mini-Speech Instructor Evaluation, 119
Instructor Evaluation Form—Ceremonial Speech, 121
Self-Evaluation Form for a Commemorative Speech, 123-124
Group Ceremonial Speaking Assignment, 125
Instructor Evaluation Form—Group Ceremonial Speaking, 127

## CHAPTER SEVEN: PUBLIC SPEAKING ANXIETY ASSIGNMENTS
Creating an Ultimate Fears List, Part 1, 130
Creating an Ultimate Fears Master List, Part 2, 131
Creating Coping Statements for Ultimate Fears, Part 3, 132
Review of Memorized Coping Statements, 133
Public Speaking Anxiety Dimensions Survey, 134
Scoring the Public Speaking Anxiety Dimensions Survey, 135
Matching Treatment to the Dimension Scores, 136
Speech Consulting Survey, 137
Final Assessment of Your Communication Apprehension, 138-139
Myself as a Communicator Paper #2, 141

## CHAPTER EIGHT: PEER FEEDBACK FORMS FOR ALL SPEECHES
Peer Feedback Instructions, 144
Peer Feedback Forms for Informative Speech #1, 145-161
Peer Feedback Forms for Informative Speech #2, 163-179
Peer Feedback Forms for Persuasive Speech #1, 181-197
Peer Feedback Forms for Persuasive Speech #2, 199-213

## CHAPTER NINE: EXTRA CREDIT
Extra Credit Speech Center Consulting Form, 217
Extra Credit Speech Evaluation, 219-222

## Appendix
Sample Persuasive Speech Outline with Highlighted Citations, 225 - 226
Presentational Slide Templates, 227-237
Speaking Card Templates, 239-245

Public Speaking Student Workbook

# 1

## COURSE POLICIES

## AND

## STUDENT INFORMATION

Chapter 1 - Information & Policies

## STUDENT INFORMATION & COURSE POLICIES
## OUTCOMES AND GOALS

**GENERAL EDUCATION**: This course fulfills the Student Learning Outcomes for Oral Communication.

**Successful students will be able to do the following:**
1. Create and develop messages demonstrating effective audience analysis and adaptation.
2. Create and develop messages demonstrating effective information gathering, analysis, and evaluation.
3. Create and deliver messages demonstrating effective organizational development and use of supporting materials from credible sources.
4. Present appropriate messages, including effective use of language, nonverbal delivery, and visual information/technology.

**COURSE GOALS**: Since communication involves both listening and speaking, the purpose of the "Public Speaking Fundamentals" course is to help you become an effective public speaker, as well as a critical listener and evaluator of public communication.

**The specific goals of this course include:**

1. To increase your understanding of the steps in the speech making process.
2. To help you view public speaking as a <u>two-way communication encounter</u> instead of a one-way performance.
3. To help you develop skills to manage communication anxiety.
4. To help you select, narrow, and design communication objectives to fit the setting, time, and audience.
5. To help you adapt your message and language to the needs and expectations of various audiences through the use of audience analysis.
6. To help you develop skills to collect, analyze, select, and use information and supporting materials (from the library and other sources) to form informative and persuasive messages.
7. To help you select and effectively use visual aids and presentational slides to enhance your informative and persuasive messages.
8. To help you organize your ideas and supporting material into coherent and captivating messages using a formal outline format.
9. To help you speak in an extemporaneous and conversational delivery style using effective gestures, body movement, voice projection, vocal variety, and eye contact.
10. To help you develop skills to speak ethically, confidently, and competently in public settings.
11. To provide opportunities for you to improve your speaking skills though practice.
12. To help you develop skills to critically listen and evaluate the public communication you encounter in daily life.

Public Speaking Student Workbook

## *COURSE POLICIES: STUDENT RESPONSIBILITIES*

**As a student in this class, you will be expected to:**

1. Be prepared for and attend each scheduled class. Since this is a skills class, attending class is an essential part of the course. Attendance will be taken every day. You are allowed 5 (MWF) or 3 (T-TH) absences (excluding speech dates or exam dates), which are intended to cover illness, physician appointments, car trouble, funerals, inclement weather, etc. After the allowed absences, 10 points for each absence may be deducted from your final point total, and every TWO tardies of 10+ minutes will count as an absence. Missing more than 9 (MWF) or 6 (T-TH) classes is grounds for FAILURE. Perfect attendance, however, may result in EXTRA CREDIT.

    a. Read all textbook and workbook pages, as assigned. Lectures may NOT mirror the assigned readings, so it is up to YOU to complete course readings on time.

    b. Bring your workbook to each class session.

2. Be a positive audience member during speeches, lectures, group activities and general class time. Disruptive or discourteous behavior may result in points being deducted from your speech grade or your dismissal from class.

    a. Participate in class discussions. However, please avoid talking while an instructor is lecturing or a student is delivering a speech.

    b. Please silence your cell phone, and do not use it in the classroom.

    c. Do not text-message during class, which is too distracting for you and others. Penalty for in-class texting is a deduction of 25 points.

    d. Do not use a laptop computer during class time unless you have special permission from your instructor.

3. Complete all written assignments ON or BEFORE the DUE DATE. Late assignments will NOT be accepted except for emergency situations. If you know you will be absent on a day an assignment is due, please give it to your instructor prior to the due date.

    a. Write or type your name on ALL assignments and complete the headings on ALL Instructor Evaluation Forms PRIOR to delivering your speeches! Failure to write your name on assignments or complete the heading on your Instructor Evaluation forms will result in a 10% loss on your grade for that assignment or speech.

    b. Type all formal preparation outlines and essays. Hand-written preparation outlines will NOT be accepted. Computers are available for speech students in the Speech Center, ASH 183, but you may only print preparation outlines

## Chapter 1 - Information & Policies

4. Complete all SPEECH ASSIGNMENTS ON or BEFORE the DUE DATE. You will be required to deliver at least FOUR formal speeches in this class, and specific requirements for each speech will be explained to you prior to each assignment.

    a. Choose speech topics and visual aids that are appropriate for a public audience. Your instructor has the right to ask you to choose an alternative topic that is more appropriate for your assignment and audience. Do NOT bring any of the following items to class: illegal substances, harmful or hazardous materials, alcohol, pornography, animals, insects, guns, knives or weapons of any kind, needles, syringes or drug paraphernalia. These items are NOT allowed on state property because they could harm others. In addition, you cannot perform any medical procedures (e.g., CPR, Heimlich maneuver, etc.) on another person in your class.

    b. When you sign up for a speaking date, that is YOUR scheduled time. LATE SPEECHES will NOT be accepted except in emergency situations. Please discuss the situation with your instructor. If you know you will be absent on a day your speech is scheduled, please make arrangements to give it prior to the due date.

    c. For each speech, you must submit a typed formal preparation outline and reference list BEFORE speaking rounds begin, or you cannot present your speech and will forfeit all points for that speech.

    d. Prior to two of your speeches, you will be required to complete an audience analysis survey of your classmates plus a tally and analysis of the results.

    e. Use appropriate language and tone during speeches and in all classroom activities. Profanity, slang, and abusive, vulgar, sexist, ethnically-biased, or irreverent language is NOT appropriate for public speaking or classroom behavior. Vulgar outbursts of anger toward the instructor or other students will result in permanent expulsion from the class.

    f. Remove your hat while speaking. Wearing a baseball cap, or any other hat, while delivering a speech, interferes with eye contact and is disrespectful to your audience. You can wear a hat while speaking ONLY if is part of a costume you are wearing as a visual aid.

    g. Discard gum before speaking. Chewing gum while delivering a speech interferes with an effective delivery and is distracting for your audience.

5. Complete all exams and quizzes on their scheduled date. Make-up exams for unexcused absences are NOT allowed except in rare cases or emergency situations. Please discuss these situations with your instructor.

6. OFFICE VISITS: Please feel free to visit with your instructor at any time during his/her office hours to discuss assignments, speech topics, speech organization, grades, as well as any other questions. Although you do NOT need an appointment during those hours, you MAY contact your instructor ahead of time to be sure he/she is available.

Public Speaking Student Workbook

## *PROFESSIONAL CLASSROOM ETIQUETTE and NETIQUETTE ASSIGNMENT*
How to Contact and Email Your Professor

**Netiquette Assignment: After reading the Classroom and Email Etiquette (Netiquette) guidelines below, please send an email to your instructor using the following guidelines.**

**Classroom Etiquette:** Courtesy and professionalism in the classroom and in relationships with your instructors implies that you respect the educational setting, the professors, and what you hope to learn. Acting in a professional manner when you contact a professor or other official demonstrates that you are taking your opportunity to pursue a college education seriously and you genuinely are seeking their help. If you desire professional consideration from your instructors, you need to follow the professional expectations that any job would require of you. Please create a positive impression when you contact your instructor by following these tips:

1. **Address your professor in a professional manner. You should never call your professor by his/her first name.** (Professors sometimes invite graduate students to call them by their first name, but undergraduates should never call an instructor by a first name.) For example, you would say or write "Hello, Mr. Jones" or "Hello, Professor Jones" or "Hello, Dr. Jones."

2. **Check the course syllabus to find your instructor's office hours and preferred method for student contact.** Your instructor will suggest drop-by times and a preferred email address or phone number. Follow what your instructor suggests.

3. **Plan to meet with your professor face-to-face if you have a concern or question about a grade.** Make an appointment with your instructor during office hours. Bring any assignments with you that are in question to show and discuss with your professor.

**Email Etiquette (Netiquette):**
1. **Use your official <u>university email account</u>** (e.g., **jmiller@unomaha.edu** NOT **crazydog@yahoo.com**) to email your professor. Other addresses may go to spam.
2. **In the <u>subject line</u>, use your first and last name, course number and time** (e.g., John Miller---CMST 1110, MW, 1 PM, so your instructor quickly identifies you.
3. **Use a <u>formal greeting</u>** to begin the email, such as, "Hello, Professor Barnes" NOT "Hey, Jo Barnes."
4. **Present your message in an organized, succinct manner.** Get to the point, such as, "Dear Dr. Barnes, I am writing to ask how many audience analysis forms I should bring to class. I missed class Monday due to illness and didn't remember if you said 20 or 25?"
5. **Conclude your email with appreciation and your name, such as,** "Thanks for your help and time, John Miller."
6. **Proofread your email before sending it.** Read it out loud and use spell-check. Remove all texting slang and abbreviations, such as LOL, CU, TY, etc.

# Chapter 1 - Information & Policies

## *ACADEMIC INTEGRITY & PLAGIARISM*

All oral and written work in Public Speaking Fundamentals must be your own. This means YOU MUST WRITE YOUR OWN SPEECHES, come up with your own topics, do your own research, organize and outline the speech yourself, and use your own wording. The word plagiarism is derived from the old English word *plagiary, which* meant literary kidnapper or thief (Webster's Dictionary, 2018). Please consider these three categories of plagiarism:

- *Global Plagiarism.* If you steal an entire speech and deliver it as your own speech, you are practicing global plagiarism.
- *Patchwriting Plagiarism.* If you steal language or ideas from several sources, patch it together, and deliver it as your own speech, you are practicing patchwriting plagiarism.
- *Incremental Plagiarism.* If you borrow quotes or paraphrases from others without giving them credit, you are practicing *incremental plagiarism* (Lucas, 2019).

The website on Academic Integrity sponsored by the Office of Academic & Student Affairs includes the following categories and definitions for *academic dishonesty:*

- **Plagiarism** is presenting the work of another as one's own (i.e. without proper acknowledgment of the source) and submitting exams, theses, reports, speeches, drawings, laboratory notes or other academic work in whole or in part as one's own when such work has been prepared by another person or copied from another person.
- **Fabrication & Falsification is** falsifying or fabricating any information or citation in any academic exercise, work, speech, or exam. Falsification is the alteration of information, while fabrication is the invention or counterfeiting of information.

**POSSIBLE PENALTIES FOR ACADEMIC DISHONESTY INCLUDE:** An "F" for the speech, exam, paper, or course and disciplinary probation.

**YOU MAY:**
1. **Discuss your topic** and/or potential research materials with others.
2. **Deliver your speech before others** and ask them to provide feedback for improving your speech. However, suggestions for improving a speech do NOT involve having someone write or rewrite entire parts of your speech.
3. **Quote from a source** or use an idea from a book, person, periodical, etc. as long as you "cite the source." Citing the source means that you acknowledge in your speech as you deliver it and in writing on your outline where you found the information and whose words you used.

**YOU MAY NOT:**
1. Deliver a speech written or previously delivered by someone else.
2. Use the ideas of others without giving them credit.
3. Use research materials, outlines, or bibliographies written by someone else.
4. Make up or invent supporting material.

## Public Speaking Student Workbook

### *CRITERIA FOR EVALUATING SPEECHES*

The following guidelines* indicate the standards that must be met in order for your speeches to earn an "A," "B," "C," "D" or "F" grade. Additionally, you must meet the requirements for each specific speaking assignment for an "A," "B," "C," or "D" grade.

**A failing (F) speech** meets any or all of the following criteria:

1. Does NOT show up to speak.
2. Plagiarizes another person's speech or sources.
3. Fabricates or falsifies supporting material.
4. Does NOT conform to the assignment in any way or form.
5. Misses the time limit by a long way (50% or more).
6. Makes NO attempt to communicate with the audience.
7. Uses profane, degrading language that humiliates or insults the audience.

**A below average (D) speech** meets any or all of the following criteria:

1. Offers the audience commonplace rather than developed or original ideas.
2. Ignores the basic strategies for organization.
3. Presents main points that are underdeveloped.
4. Uses little or NO supporting material (or citations for sources).
5. Reads the speech and/or ignores the audience.
6. Completely disregards the time limit for the speech.

**An average (C) speech** meets the following criteria:

1. Conforms to the assignment (informative, persuasive).
2. Uses a clear introduction and conclusion (although both could be more engaging or developed).
3. Uses a clearly stated purpose and identifiable main points.
4. Supports points with interesting information (although may use only a minimum number of citations).
5. Sounds conversational (but might read large portions of the speech).
6. Uses some effective nonverbal physical delivery--at least a little movement, gesturing, facial expression, and eye contact (although may also use some distracting mannerisms).
7. Conforms to or comes close to the time limit.

*The guidelines for the "A," "B," and "C" speech are loosely based on the never-aging standards for speech delivery suggested by R. Oliver in *The Speech Teacher (1960-1)*.

**An above average (B) speech** meets the criteria for a "C" speech plus:

1. Demonstrates clear organizational skills in the introduction, body, and conclusion.
2. Clearly amplifies main points with interesting supporting material.
3. Uses language in an interesting manner.
4. Clearly adapts the topic to the audience.
5. Sounds extemporaneous and conversational, maintaining the audience's interest.
6. Uses some effective nonverbal physical delivery--movement, gesturing, facial expression, and sustained eye contact.
7. Conforms to the time limit.

**An excellent (A) speech** meets all the criteria for a "B" speech plus:

1. Demonstrates creativity in selecting and developing a topic worthy of the audience's time and attention.
2. Presents carefully selected, appropriate, and convincing supporting material adapted to the audience's needs.
3. Uses clear, vivid, and motivating language that is appropriate for the audience, topic, and occasion.
4. Incorporates effective, appropriate, and/or captivating vocal variety and nonverbal physical delivery--movement, gestures, facial expression, and well-sustained eye contact with the audience.
5. Maintains the audience's interest throughout the speech and involves the audience in the issues presented.
6. Establishes strong speaker credibility based on clear thinking, well-supported ideas or assertions, and logical reasoning.
7. Displays poise and confidence in an extemporaneous and conversational delivery.
8. Succeeds at enlightening the audience or moving them toward agreement with the speaker's central idea.

**In summary**, a speech that merits a:
"D" grade is underdeveloped and lacks appropriate supporting materials, organization, and extemporaneous delivery.

"C" grade is well-packaged but lacks audience impact, convincing supporting materials, sustained eye contact, and effective nonverbal delivery.

"B" grade demonstrates clear signs of thinking, acting, and engaging the audience, but needs additional work in developing ideas and improving delivery.

"A" grade has virtually all the skills needed for effective delivery of ideas, beliefs, attitudes, values, and/or behaviors.

Public Speaking Student Workbook

## *STUDENT INFORMATION SHEET*

Please complete the following information. It will help your instructor become acquainted with you, as well as provide information in case your instructor needs to contact you during the semester (for reasons involving illness, emergencies, etc.).

1.  Name: _____ Student ID #: _____
2.  Preferred Name: _____ Class Time: _____
3.  Local Address (& Zip Code): _____
4.  E-mail Address: _____
5.  High School Attended & Graduation Date: _____
6.  Year in College: _____ College Major: _____
7.  Did you take a speech course in high school? ___ If yes, when (e.g., 11th grade)? _____
8.  Was a public speaking course <u>required</u> in high school? ____ Did you learn public speaking skills in any other high school course? ____ Which course (e.g., English)? ___
9.  Did you learn public speaking skills in any other setting or club? ____ If yes, where? (e.g., Forensics team, 4-H Club)? _____
10. How many *formal public speeches have you given in a school setting?
11. How many *formal public speeches have you given in any other setting (work, club)?
12. Describe how developing public speaking skills can help you further your career goal: _____
13. Describe your worst fear(s) about public speaking: _____
14. Please share any other information you think your instructor should know about you that is pertinent to this course: _____
15. Please write any questions you have about this class (use the back side of this page).
16. "I have read & I understand the course policies & requirements explained on pages 4-8 in this workbook." Please sign your name in the space below.

   _____ Date _____

* Note: A formal public speech means you stood in front of 15 or more people and gave a prepared speech.

Chapter 1 - Information & Policies

## *MYSELF AS A COMMUNICATOR PAPER #1*

1. Please describe how you see yourself as a "communicator" in the following situations:

    a. In Everyday Conversations:

    b. In Class or Group Discussions:

    c. In Meetings:

    d. In Public Speaking:

    e. Overall (in most situations):

2. Please describe where in your body you experience anxiety about speaking in public (stomach butterflies, racing heart, sweating, shaking limbs, mind—forgetting points, mind—thinking negative thoughts, blushing, etc.):

# 2

# MANAGING
# PUBLIC SPEAKING ANXIETY

Chapter 2 - Managing Public Speaking Anxiety

## *CONQUERING SPEECH ANXIETY*
## *JOURNAL ASSIGNMENT*

**Objectives**
1. To record your reactions to activities and techniques covered in class.
2. To evaluate your own progress over the semester by reviewing your journal entries.
3. To provide feedback to your instructor about the helpfulness of techniques and your
progress in overcoming speech anxiety.

**Explanation**
The journal is your opportunity to share your comments and feelings about the class activities. You should write a few paragraphs in your journal after every class period and after any other class-related activity that you practice at home. Each journal entry should include the following information:

Date:

Description of Class Activity or Technique:

Practical Application Comment (Did you like it? Did you understand it? Do you think it has possibilities for reducing your CA if you practice it more? Explain.):

Change in Your CA Level (Are you experiencing any alleviation in your CA level? How are you feeling about speaking in public now?):

(OPTIONAL) Suggestions for Future Classroom Use (Include any suggestions for the instructor regarding use in future classes.):

**Evaluation Criteria**
The journals will be collected three times during the semester. This assignment will be UNGRADED. You will receive up to 15 daily assignment points for writing your journal entries. Since a journal is an opportunity to freely record your thoughts, grammar or punctuation will not be evaluated.

**First Journal Entry**: How I See Myself as a Communicator Today
Please describe how you see yourself as a communicator on this first day of class in the following situations (See Workbook p. 10):

1. Public speaking opportunities,
2. Group or classroom discussions,
3. Meetings, and
4. Interpersonal conversations.

## MANAGING FEAR, NERVOUSNESS, AND ANXIETY ABOUT PUBLIC SPEAKING

Fear, anxiety, uneasiness or nervousness about communication are words often used interchangeably with the scholarly term "communication apprehension" (CA for short). James McCroskey (2005) author of An Introduction to Rhetorical Communication defines CA as: "an individual's level of fear or anxiety associated with either real or anticipated communication with another person or persons."

CA is a common emotional response to public speaking that many experience. In fact, recent research involving thousands of college students and adults indicates that between 60% to 75% of our population reports a fear or anxiety about public speaking (Davidson & Dwyer, 2012; McCroskey, 2005; Richmond & McCroskey, 1998). That means almost three out of every four people around you would say they are anxious or nervous when it comes to giving a speech. Consequently, if you thought you were the only one whoever experienced anxiety about public speaking, now you know that a majority of those around you may experience a similar emotion.

The skills you will learn in this class and the opportunities you will have to practice delivering speeches will help reduce much of your apprehension. In addition, your textbook and this workbook will give you some important tips on how to manage your nervousness.

The following survey, called McCroskey's Personal Report of Communication Apprehension (PRCA-24) (Richmond, et al., 1998) will help you assess your overall CA level, as well as your CA level for each of four contexts--including group discussions, meetings, interpersonal conversations, and public speaking. Directions for self-scoring your answers will follow the questions.

Dwyer, K. K., & Davidson, M. M. (2012). Is public speaking really more feared than death?
*Communication Research Reports, 29*(2), 99-107.

McCroskey, J. (2005). *An introduction to rhetorical communication (9th ed.).* Boston: Allen & Bacon.

Richmond, V., Wrench, J., & McCroskey, J. (2013). *Communication: Apprehension, avoidance, and effectiveness (6th ed.).* Boston: Pearson.

# Chapter 2 - Managing Public Speaking Anxiety

## *ASSESSING YOUR COMMUNICATION APPREHENSION LEVEL*

Name: _____ ID#: _____ Date: _____

McCroskey's Personal Report of Communication Apprehension (PRCA-24) *

Directions: This instrument is composed of twenty-four statements concerning feelings about communicating with others. Work quickly, record your first impression. Please <u>indicate in the space provided the degree to which each statement applies to you by marking</u>:

**(1) Strongly Agree  (2) Agree  (3) Are Undecided  (4) Disagree  (5) Strongly Disagree**

____ 1. I dislike participating in group discussions.
____ 2. Generally, I am comfortable while participating in group discussions.
____ 3. I am tense and nervous while participating in group discussions.
____ 4. I like to get involved in group discussions.
____ 5. Engaging in a group discussion with new people makes me tense and nervous.
____ 6. I am calm and relaxed while participating in group discussions.
____ 7. Generally, I am nervous when I have to participate in a meeting.
____ 8. Usually, I am calm and relaxed while participating in a meeting.
____ 9. I am very calm and relaxed when I am called upon to express an opinion at a meeting.
____ 10. I am afraid to express myself at meetings.
____ 11. Communicating at meetings usually makes me uncomfortable.
____ 12. I am very relaxed when answering questions at a meeting.
____ 13. While participating in a conversation with a new acquaintance, I feel very nervous.
____ 14. I have no fear of speaking up in conversations.
____ 15. Ordinarily I am very tense and nervous in conversations.
____ 16. Ordinarily I am very calm and relaxed in conversations.
____ 17. While conversing with a new acquaintance, I feel very relaxed.
____ 18. I'm afraid to speak up in conversations.
____ 19. I have no fear of giving a speech.
____ 20. Certain parts of my body feel very tense and rigid while I am giving a speech.
____ 21. I feel relaxed while giving a speech.
____ 22. My thoughts become confused and jumbled when I am giving a speech.
____ 23. I face the prospect of giving a speech with confidence.
____ 24. While giving a speech, I get so nervous I forget facts I really know.

# Public Speaking Student Workbook
## *SCORING & INTERPRETING YOUR SCORES*

Name_____ Date: _____

**SCORING**: To compute your scores, please add or subtract your scores for each item as indicated below. (Please note that "18" is a constant so all your sub-scores will be computed by starting with a total of "18".)

**Sub-score (Context)**            **Scoring Formula**

**Group Discussions**:  18 plus + scores for items 2____, 4____, & 6____; minus (-) scores for items 1____, 3____, & 5____ = *_____.

**Meetings**:  18 plus + scores for items 8____, 9____, & 12____; minus(-) scores for items 7____, 10____, & 11____ = *_____.

**Interpersonal**:  18 plus + scores for items 14____, 16____, & 17____; minus (-) scores for items 13____, 15____, & 18____ = *_____.

**Public Speaking**:  18 plus+ scores for items 19____, 21____, & 23____; minus (-) for items 20____, 22____, & 24____ = *_____.

**Overall**:  Add all four sub-scores: *Group Discussions + *Meetings + *Interpersonal Conversations + *Public Speaking = _____.

Using the scoring formulas, please compute your five scores above and write them in the following chart under YOUR SCORE.

### YOUR PRCA SCORES CHART

| OVERALL & CONTEXT | YOUR SCORE | "" CHECK YOUR LEVEL / RANGE |||
|---|---|---|---|---|
| | | LOW | AVERAGE | HIGH |
| **Group** | _____ | _____ | _____ | _____ |
| **Meetings** | _____ | _____ | _____ | _____ |
| **Interpersonal** | _____ | _____ | _____ | _____ |
| **Public Speaking** | _____ | _____ | _____ | _____ |
| **Overall** | _____ | _____ | _____ | _____ |

INTERPRETING: To interpret your scores, you can compare your scores with the thousands of people who have also completed the PRCA-24 (see Norms Chart on the next page).

## Chapter 2 - Managing Public Speaking Anxiety

### *NORMS CHART FOR THE PRCA-24*

| CONTEXT & OVERALL | AVERAGE SCORE | AVERAGE RANGE | HIGH CA SCORES |
|---|---|---|---|
| Group | 15.4 | 11 to 20 | 21 & ABOVE |
| Meeting | 16.4 | 12 to 21 | 22 & ABOVE |
| Interpersonal | 14.5 | 10 to 18 | 19 & ABOVE |
| Public Speaking | 19.3 | 14 to 24 | 25 & ABOVE |
| Overall | 65.6 | 50 to 80 | 81 & ABOVE |

The OVERALL SCORE can range from 24 to 120. According to McCroskey, the average overall score is 65.6 and the average range of scores is 50 to 80. If your overall score is near 65, then it is about normal. If it falls between 50 and 80, it may be a bit above average or below average, but it is still within the normal range. If your OVERALL SCORE is above 80, you can conclude that you have a higher-than-average level of CA. If your OVERALL SCORE is below 50, you can conclude that you have a lower-than-average level of CA.

Scores for each of the four contexts--GROUP DISCUSSIONS, MEETINGS, INTERPERSONAL CONVERSATIONS, and PUBLIC SPEAKING--can range from 6 to 30. According to McCroskey, any subscore above 18 indicates you have some degree of communication apprehension in a specific context. Notice that the average public speaking score is above 18 thus indicates most people tend to be apprehensive about public speaking.

Now return to "Your PRCA Scores Chart" on the previous page and CHECK (✓) the level for each of your scores in comparison to the "Norms Chart." This chart will give you a good assessment of your overall and context CA levels. If your overall CA score and/or context scores are in the HIGH CA range, you should discuss your scores with your instructor to get additional suggestions for reducing CA. Additionally, you should try to learn and practice the Cognitive Restructuring Technique (especially the Positive Coping Statements) and the Deep Abdominal Breathing Exercise explained on the following pages.

Public Speaking Student Workbook

## *THE COGNITIVE RESTRUCTURING TECHNIQUE: PART ONE*
### *Discovering and Disconnecting Anxious Thoughts*

**OBJECTIVES:**
1. To discover or recognize the fears and unproductive thoughts you have about public speaking.
2. To develop truthful coping statements to <u>replace</u> your fears and anxious thoughts about public speaking.

**INSTRUCTIONS:**
More than 60% to 75% (Richmond & McCroskey, 1998, Dwyer & Davidson, 2012) of adults and college students report that they fear public speaking. One study reported many Americans list a fear of public speaking more often then they list a fear of death. So, if you have fears about public speaking, you are NOT alone. Great speakers, musicians, athletes, and performers often reveal they have butterflies and performance anxiety. However, experienced speakers and performers have learned to manage or conquer these fears. You too can learn techniques to help reduce your anxiety about public speaking. One technique called "cognitive restructuring" will help you learn new coping statements to replace anxious thoughts about public speaking.

**REQUIREMENTS**:

**PART ONE.** The first step in cognitive restructuring is to create an Anxious Thoughts and Fears List. Consider a time in the past when you had to deliver a speech or speak in front of a group of people. Using the space below, list at least 5 OR MORE of your fears, anxieties or worries about delivering a speech. (i.e., What makes you anxious about giving a speech? What is the worst that could happen? What are your negative thoughts about presenting to an audience?)

### **ANXIOUS THOUGHTS AND FEARS LIST**

Fear #1:

Fear #2:

Fear #3:

Fear #4:

Fear #5:

Dwyer, K. K., & Davidson, M. M. (2012). Is public speaking really more feared than death? *Communication Research Reports, 29*(2), 99-107.

## Chapter 2 - Managing Public Speaking Anxiety

**PART TWO.** The second step in cognitive restructuring is to identify those anxious thoughts and fears on your list that are unproductive and untrue. To do this, look through the following list of unproductive thoughts and identify (✓) the ones that pertain to your Ultimate Fears List.

### UNPRODUCTIVE THOUGHTS LIST *
### (THOUGHTS THAT WORK AGAINST YOU AND GIVE YOU ANXIETY)

"✓"

__1) **Unrealistic Self-Expectations and "Must" Thinking**: I must be perfect. I must give a perfect speech. I must never make a mistake. I must always appear in control.
**The Truth**: No one will ever be perfect in this life. We are all fallible humans who make mistakes. No one expects perfection from you. You only have to give your best effort. Public speaking class is designed to help you try out your skills and to make adjustments.

__2) **Excessive Fear of Disapproval**: No one will like me or my speech. Everyone will be bored listening to me or know more about the topic than me. The audience might think I'm stupid.
**The Truth**: Some will appreciate your ideas. You only need to prepare and offer what you can. If you have researched your topic, you will know more about the topic than most people in class. Your enthusiasm will be contagious and interest others.

__3) **Anticipating the Worst Outcome or Playing the Psychic**: I will never give a good speech. No one will like what I say. I know I will make mistakes and the audience will notice every mistake I make. I'll probably forget some part of my speech and be a failure. **The Truth**: You cannot predict the future. If you prepare your speech outline, you will have notes to guide you. If you make a mistake or forget a part, you can refer to your notes and keep going. Even the best speakers make mistakes, correct themselves, and keep going.

__4) **Believing the Audience is Hyper-Critical**: Everyone is judging every detail about me. If my audience sees me sweat, stumble, shake or blush, they will think I am a failure, and I will look like a fool. Everyone in the class is a better speaker than I am. **The Truth**: Your audience is listening for helpful ideas. They are far less critical than you are of yourself. You feel nervousness from the inside. Your audience cannot feel your heartbeat and will NOT notice the nervousness you feel. They are students, like you.

__5) **Emotional Reasoning**: I'm getting nervous; I can feel it. It's going to be a terrible speech. I'm the only one who is this nervous. I'm going to get a bad grade.
**The Truth**: A little nervous activation is normal. Everyone experiences it. It can add to your enthusiasm. It should NOT determine your thoughts. Focusing on your message instead of your nervousness will cause nervous feelings to subside as you deliver your speech. Preparing, organizing, and practicing will help you get a good grade.

__6) **Viewing Public Speaking from a Performance Perspective**: I must become something other than I am to be a successful public speaker. Public speaking demands perfect, formal, flawless, and eloquent oratorical skills. **The Truth**: Public speaking is a communication encounter; it relies on communication skills that you use in everyday conversation. The focus is on helping the audience understand your message. You can be yourself and use your natural conversational delivery.

**PART THREE.** The third step in cognitive restructuring is to create a new list of truthful coping statements to replace the old unproductive thoughts you have been thinking. The following list of positive coping statements can replace many of your unproductive thoughts. Read through this list and check (✓) the ones that pertain to YOUR Ultimate Fears List in Part TWO.

Public Speaking Student Workbook

## *POSITIVE COPING STATEMENTS\**
*(Thoughts That Work for You and Reduce Anxiety)*

"√"

_1) Public speaking is a communication encounter, NOT a magnified performance. My main goal is to clearly communicate my message. I can and will use the same conversational style I use daily with family and friends. I can be myself.

_2) Since I am able to speak without nervousness in many situations involving my friends or family, I can speak without nervousness in front of the students in my class who have experienced the same anxiety about public speaking as I do.

_3) The audience is NOT evaluating my every word or every hair on my head. Fellow students in my audience are like myself; they are simply looking for helpful ideas that can aid or enrich their lives in some way. They will listen and be supportive.

_4) Everyone experiences some degree of anxiety or nervousness when speaking in front of others. Feeling a bit of nervousness will NOT keep me from speaking. Such feelings are a sign that I am enthusiastic and "psyched up" to give my speech.

_5) Worry only agitates and demoralizes a person. I have no need to worry about my speech because I will contribute something by planning, researching, and sharing my ideas. My preparation and organization contribute most to earning a good grade.

_6) Audiences seldom notice nervousness; they can't feel my heart beat. Focusing on my fears or feelings of nervousness will only prevent me from concentrating on my presentation. I will direct my attention to communicating the points in my speech.

_7) No one is perfect or fully competent in all aspects of life. I do not have to be perfect or give a perfect speech. Like me, everyone in this class is learning and practicing new public speaking skills. I only have to give my best effort in preparation, practice and delivery.

_8) If I lose my place in my speech or forget something, it is not a catastrophe. Most people won't even notice. My audience will wait while I look at my notes and move onto my next point. Even the best speakers make mistakes and go on and so will I.

_9) If I research my topic and prepare my speech, I will sound knowledgeable. I will probably know more about the topic than most people in the class. My enthusiasm will be contagious and interest others in the topic.

_10) Blaming myself for past shortcomings or failures will NOT foster my goals. I will learn positive coping statements to replace my unproductive thoughts and negative thinking. This WILL help reduce my communication anxiety and nervousness.

_11) Even if I feel some anxiety, I will act as if I am NOT anxious. I will believe in myself and my goals to help others. I will use self-talk that is confident, not nerve-wracking.

*"The Cognitive Restructuring Technique" is adapted from exercises in the book, IConquer Speech Anxiety, 2020, KLD Books Inc., by Karen Kangas Dwyer.*

## Chapter 2 - Managing Public Speaking Anxiety

**PART FOUR.** The fourth step in cognitive restructuring is to memorize and practice your coping statements so that you have a new script in your mind to replace your old unproductive thoughts. You should memorize the coping statements that apply most to your unproductive thoughts or create your own personal coping statements from a combination of positive coping statements. In summary, you should:

1. Read through your personal list of coping statements every day or until you know it by heart. Try to read it aloud so you feel a connection with each of your coping statements. You may want to post your coping statements list on a mirror where you dress, on a refrigerator, or other conspicuous place where you can be reminded to read your list often.

2. Practices using coping statements to diminish your anxiety as you prepare to give each speech. The moment you feel anxious about public speaking, recognize the unproductive thoughts you have been thinking and then confront them with your coping statements. Practice your coping statements until they automatically replace your unproductive thoughts.

3. Don't be discouraged if your old unproductive thoughts keep popping in your mind. You have been thinking some of those thoughts for a long time. It will take a few weeks of diligent practice to disconnect automatic unproductive thoughts. So be heartened and know that your efforts will be rewarded with practice.

### THE FORMULA FOR BUILDING CONFIDENCE IN PUBLIC SPEAKING

Researchers in the field of communication point out that most anxiety about public speaking comes from a speaker's thoughts about himself/herself in the situation. The more you believe you have the knowledge and skills to give a good speech, the more you will approach giving a speech with eagerness and confidence. This course is designed to teach the skills that can help every student develop confidence about public speaking. Therefore, it is important that you attend class and complete every assignment. As you do, you will become more confident.
(See the two contrasting formulas below.)

**Formula #1:**
Attend Class + Preparation + Research + Practice = SUCCESS AND CONFIDENCE

**Formula #2:**
Skip Class + Procrastination + Little or NO Research + Little or NO Preparation + Little or NO Practice = FAILURE AND MORE ANXIETY

Public Speaking Student Workbook

## *DIAPHRAGMATIC BREATHING EXERCISE FOR REDUCING TENSENESS & ANXIETY*

**OBJECTIVE**:
To help reduce tenseness and to help you feel calm before giving a speech.

**INSTRUCTIONS**:
Diaphragmatic breathing (deep abdominal breathing) is a calming exercise you can do any time you feel anxious or tense, especially before delivering a speech. Just three (3) minutes of diaphragmatic breathing can help reduce tenseness or nervousness and bring on relaxation. You can practice it either standing or sitting. Follow these steps:

1. First, scan your body and note if you are feeling any tenseness or anxiety.

2. Next, find your rib cage and place one hand directly below your rib cage--that is, your ABDOMEN.

3. Practice exhaling long breaths through your mouth making a *whoooo* sound, like the blowing wind, and allowing your abdomen to pull inward

4. Now, inhale <u>slowly and deeply</u> through your nose, feeling your abdomen expand and your hand rise for a count of four (1-2-3-4-). Your chest should barely move.

5. Pause slightly and smile for a count of four (1, 2, 3, 4). Smiling releases endorphins (natural mood elevators) into your blood.

6. Then, exhale slowly and fully through your mouth, making the *whoooo* sound for a slow count of four (1-2-3-4-).

7. Relax and take a few normal breaths. Tell your body to go loose and limp. Make an effort to let all tension drain away from every part of your body.

8. Continue taking at least fifteen to twenty deep abdominal breaths with slow, full exhales in order to trigger relaxation.

**TIPS**:
1. Try to keep your breathing smooth and regular. Try not to gulp the air.

2. Try to practice diaphragmatic breathing at least three to five minutes (about 10 deep breaths) every day. It will help reduce anxiety and induce feelings of calmness.

3. You can adjust this exercise so you can perform it without others noticing. Simply exhale through your nose, instead of making the wind sound through your mouth.

4. If you get a little lightheaded at first, from the increased supply of oxygen, simply return to regular breathing for a minute or two.

# Chapter 2 - Managing Public Speaking Anxiety

# 3

## GETTING STARTED

## INTRODUCTORY MINI SPEECHES

## SPEECH PREPARATION AIDS

# Chapter 3 - Getting Started

Public Speaking Student Workbook
*MY PERSONA MINI-SPEECH
INTRODUCTION ASSIGNMENT*

## OBJECTIVES

1. To share information about yourself so the class will become acquainted with you.
2. To practice speaking in front of the class in a non-threatening format.

## INSTRUCTIONS

The "My Persona" assignment is a short 1 to 2-minute mini-speech in which you tell the audience about one of your most familiar topics—YOURSELF! Plan to develop and organize your speech by addressing these three parts:

Past: State your name. Describe where you were born, the size of your family, interesting places you have lived or visited, and/or any special achievements you have attained.

Present: Describe your year in college, your major, your hobbies, your present job, and/or any other important things in your life.

Future: Describe your future career or lifetime goals and/or any other special plans you hope to accomplish. Restate your name.

## EXPECTATIONS & EVALUATION CRITERIA

1. Prepare your presentation by jotting down notes that fit each part of the speech, described above. Try to choose information that you think will be somewhat interesting to your classmates. Next, read over your notes and determine what you want to share that will fit in the 1 to a 2-minute time limit. Then on an index card (5" x 8"), write down key words or points to jog your memory while delivering your speech. Practice your speech with your cards so that you know it well and know it fits the time requirements.

2. Practice your coping statements (see Workbook p. 19) prepare your mini-speech and as you come to class on the day of your presentation.

3. When you give your presentation, you will walk to the front of the room and place your card on the lectern. Try to make a special effort to speak conversationally and loud enough so all can hear you and to look at some member(s) of your audience. SMILE.

4. You will receive ___ points for delivering the mini-speech, fulfilling the time requirement, and covering the three aspects of your life.

# Chapter 3 - Getting Started

## *INSTRUCTOR FEEDBACK CHECKLIST for MINI-SPEECH #1*

SPEAKER: _____ DATE: _____ CLASS TIME: _____

_____ (%) POINTS EARNED

PAST:
___ A stated name
___ Described birthplace & family
___ Described achievements &/or travels

PRESENT:
___ Described college year & major
___ Described job & hobbies
___ Described other important aspects

FUTURE:
___ Described goals & plans
___ Restated name

DELIVERY:
___ Placed note card on lectern
___ Smiled occasionally at audience
___ Looked at some members of audience while speaking
___ Glanced only occasionally at notes
___ Sounded extemporaneous (not memorized or read)
___ Sounded conversational
___ Projected voice so all could hear (__ Spoke too softly __ Spoke too loudly)
___ Used appropriate & audience-inclusive language (__ Avoided slang and profanity)

OVERALL REQUIREMENTS:
___ Fulfilled 1 to 2-minute time requirement (__ Too short __ Too long)

COMMENTS:

Public Speaking Student Workbook

## *THE COLLEAGUE INTRODUCTION MINI-SPEECH*
## *INTRODUCTION ASSIGNMENT – OPTION #2*

**OBJECTIVES**
1. To interview and introduce a classmate so the class can become acquainted with him/her.
2. To practice speaking in front of the class in a non-threatening format.

**INSTRUCTIONS**
The "Colleague Introduction" assignment is a short 1 to 2-minute mini-speech in which you will introduce a classmate to the class. You should pair off with a person you have NOT met. Interview your partner and take notes about information shared. Plan your interview questions so you can develop and organize your speech by addressing these three parts:

Past:     State your partner's preferred name and an interesting fact about him/her. Describe where he/she was born, the family size, interesting places he/she has lived or visited, and any special achievements attained.

Present:  Describe his/her year in college, major, hobbies, present job, and/or any other important things or experiences in his/her life.

Future:   Describe his/her future career or lifetime goals and any other special plans he/she hopes to accomplish. Restate his/her name.

**EXPECTATIONS & EVALUATION CRITERIA**
1. After interviewing your partner in class, read over your notes. Prepare your presentation to fit each part of the speech, described above. Try to choose information that you think will be interesting to your classmates and will fit in the 1 to 2-minute time limit. (Also, try to be creative in the beginning of your speech. For example, instead of saying, "This is so and so," you might begin: "Have you ever wondered what it is like to drive an ambulance? My new friend John Doe can tell you what it's like because he's a paramedic.") Then on an index card (5" x 8"), write down key words to jog your memory while delivering your speech. Practice your speech with your cards so that you know it fits the time requirements.

2. When you give your presentation, walk to the front of the room with your partner. (Your partner may stand or sit on a chair next to the podium.) Place your card on the lectern. Try to make a special effort to speak conversationally and loud enough so all can hear you. Try to look at some member(s) of your audience while speaking. SMILE. Glance only occasionally at your notes.

3. You will receive ___ points for delivering the mini-speech, fulfilling the time requirement, and covering the three aspects of your partner's life.

# Chapter 3 - Getting Started

## *INSTRUCTOR FEEDBACK and CHECKLIST for MINI-SPEECH #2*

SPEAKER: _____ DATE: _____ CLASS TIME: _____

_____ (%) POINTS EARNED

### PAST:
___ Creative introduction
___ Stated partner's name
___ Described birthplace & family
___ Described achievements/ travels

### PRESENT:
___ Described college year & major
___ Described job & hobbies
___ Described other important aspects

### FUTURE:
___ Described goals & plans
___ Restated partner's name

### DELIVERY & EXPRESSION:
___ Placed note card on lectern
___ Smiled occasionally at audience
___ Looked at some members of audience while speaking
___ Glanced only occasionally at notes
___ Sounded extemporaneous (not memorized or read)
___ Sounded conversational
___ Projected voice so all could hear (__ Spoke too softly __ Spoke too loudly)
___ Used appropriate & audience-inclusive language (__ Avoided slang or profanity)

### OVERALL REQUIREMENTS:
___ Fulfilled 1 to 2-minute time requirement (__ Too short __ Too long)

### COMMENTS:

Public Speaking Student Workbook

## *THE LEISURE TIME & VISUAL AID MINI-SPEECH*

**OBJECTIVES**
1. To practice using visual aids while delivering a speech.
2. To practice organizing, preparing, and delivering a speech.

**INSTRUCTIONS**
The "Leisure Time & Visual Aid" assignment is a short 1 to 2-minute mini-speech in which you tell the audience about one of your most familiar topics - YOURSELF plus your leisure-time activities. Plan to bring a few (2 to 3) small or portable visual aids in a large brown paper bag to help explain how you spend your spare time (e.g., a tennis racket for playing tennis, a game piece for Chess, a favorite book for reading, etc.). Plan to develop your speech by addressing these three parts:

Introduction: State your name, where you were born or grew up, the size of your family, any special achievements you have attained, your year in college, your major, and your job. Describe how much leisure time you find in a day or week and how many objects you brought with you to explain your leisure time activities.

Body: One at a time, pull the objects from the bag. Holding or displaying each one, describe how it explains what you like to do with your leisure time.

Conclusion: Signal ending and say, "in conclusion." Explain what your choices for spare time activities reveal about your personality and/or your life. Then restate your name.

**EXPECTATIONS & EVALUATION CRITERIA**
1. Choose visual aids that fit the assignment and are portable in the brown bag. Prepare your presentation by jotting down notes that fit each part of the speech, described above. Next, read over your notes and determine what will fit in the 1 to 2-minute time limit. On an index card (5" x 8"), write down key words to jog your memory while delivering your speech. Practice your speech with your cards and visual aids so that you know it fits the time requirements.

2. BRING YOUR VISUAL AIDS WITH YOU TO CLASS IN A BAG. When you give your speech, walk to the front of the room and place your card on the lectern. Try to make a special effort to speak loud enough so all can hear you and to display your visual aid(s) so all can see. In addition, try to speak conversationally and look at your audience, NOT your visual aid. SMILE. Glance only occasionally at your notes.

3. You will receive 10 points for delivering the Leisure Time & Visual Aid Mini-speech, using visual aids effectively, fulfilling the time requirement, and covering the three parts in the outline.

# Chapter 3 - Getting Started

## *INSTRUCTOR FEEDBACK and CHECKLIST*

SPEAKER: _____ DATE: _____ CLASS TIME: _____

_____ (%) POINTS EARNED

### INTRODUCTION:
___ State your name, home town (where you grew up), major, & year in college
___ Identified how much & when you find leisure time
___ Described how many objects you brought to explain leisure time activities

### BODY & VISUAL AIDS:
___ Displayed objects one at a time as you described what you like to do with your leisure time
___ Displayed objects so all could see them

### CONCLUSION:
___ Signaled ending with "In conclusion"
___ Explained what your spare time choices reveal about your life and personality

### DELIVERY & EXPRESSION:
___ Placed note card on lectern
___ Smiled occasionally at audience
___ Looked at some members of audience while speaking
___ Glanced only occasionally at notes
___ Sounded extemporaneous (not memorized or read)
___ Sounded conversational
___ Projected voice so all could hear (__ Spoke too softly __ Spoke too loudly)
___ Used appropriate & audience-inclusive language (__ Avoided slang or profanity)

### OVERALL REQUIREMENTS:
___ Fulfilled 1 to 2-minute time requirement  (__ Too short __ Too long)

### COMMENTS:

Public Speaking Student Workbook
*TOPIC SELECTION EXERCISE*

NAME: _____ CLASS TIME: _____

*CLUSTERING AND BRAINSTORMING*

List five (5) items in each category that you know about and/or are interested in/willing to research. Avoid common topics such as LeBron James, the president, drunk driving, and smoking. Be creative!

| People | Events | Concepts/Ideas |
|---|---|---|
| 1. | 1. | 1. |
| 2. | 2. | 2. |
| 3. | 3. | 3. |
| 4. | 4. | 4. |
| 5. | 5. | 5. |

| Places/Travel | Nature/Weather | Hobbies/Sports |
|---|---|---|
| 1. | 1. | 1. |
| 2. | 2. | 2. |
| 3. | 3. | 3. |
| 4. | 4. | 4. |
| 5. | 5. | 5. |

| Work/Career/Major | Process/How To | Problems/Concerns |
|---|---|---|
| 1. | 1. | 1. |
| 2. | 2. | 2. |
| 3. | 3. | 3. |
| 4. | 4. | 4. |
| 5. | 5. | 5 |

*NARROWING YOUR TOPIC*

Create subtopics by taking your favorite four (4) topics from the categories above. Compose sub-lists under each topic by listing three (3) or more narrowed items. Your final list should include 12 items.

| Original Topic | Sub Topic #1 | Sub Topic #2 | Sub Topic #3 |
|---|---|---|---|
| 1. | | | |
| 2. | | | |
| 3. | | | |
| 4. | | | |

# Chapter 3 - Getting Started
## *IDEAS FOR INFORMATIVE SPEECHES*

Use this list as a way to brainstorm for your own ideas. **Creative** ideas result in interesting and effective speeches!

**Topics for a Process**
- Apply contouring makeup
- Aromatherapy
- Assemble a skateboard
- Athletic training
- Autism
- Balance a monthly budget
- Clean an instrument
- Car repair
- Cross-stitch
- Design a bouquet
- Start a blog
- Draw cartoon characters
- Fix drywall
- Flip a House
- Flotation therapy
- Fold an American flag

Give your car a tune-up
- Plan an inexpensive date
- Groom a dog
- History of UNO
- Interview preparation
- Interior Design
- Jumpstart a car
- Make a clay vase
- Make a candle
- Make an origami figure
- Make Crab Rangoon
- Manage stress
- Personality types
- Play poker
- Play an instrument
- Play tennis
- Counterfeit money
- Remove scratch from a car
- Sail a boat
- Save at the grocery store
- Screen-print t-shirts
- Skydive
- Snowboard
- Start from sprinting blocks
- Pilot an airplane
- Take a perfect Selfie
- Throw a curve ball
- Tune a guitar
- Write a poem
- Work as a Barista

**Concepts, Objects, Events**
- African Music
- Anorexia Nervosa
- American Sign Language
- Arbor Day
- Anger management
- Bed Bugs
- Black history in textbooks
- Chemical Weapons
- Cloud systems
- Comic books
- Dr. Seuss
- Egyptian Pharaohs
- Elvis Presley
- Evolution of manners
- Gaming
- Hippie Movement
- History of athletic shoes
- History of Tattoos
- Hot Wheels cars
- Great Barrier Reef
- Insomnia
- Mayan Empire
- Laughter
- Legos
- Little Rock Nine
- Mann's Chinese Theater
- Monopoly (board game)
- New York Yankees
- Nikola Tesla
- North Korea
- Obsessive-Compulsive disorder
- Online degrees
- Optical illusions
- Parachuting
- Pugs
- Rally racing
- Rappelling
- Silly putty
- Sleeping disorders
- Sports officials
- Study abroad programs
- Jimmy Fallon
- Tornadoes
- Vertical ice climbing
- Warren Buffet

- Wilderness Therapy
- Winston Churchill
- Wonders of the World

How Things Work:
- Hydrogen fuel cells
- Drones
- Lasik eye surgery
- Microwaves
- Nuclear reactors
- EMPs

**Choose Subjects for Classroom Speeches Topics that YOU:**

1. Know a lot about and/or have experience with;

2. Will investigate and research because you are interested in them; and

3. Care about or are passionate about (especially for persuasive speeches).

Additionally, always consider your audience's needs and interests.

Public Speaking Student Workbook

## *PURPOSE AND CENTRAL IDEA GUIDELINES*

The specific purpose is a brief statement of your goal for your speech.
The central idea is a brief, one-sentence summary of the points (or main ideas) in your speech.

### *Guidelines for Writing a Specific Purpose*

(Note: Please use these guidelines as they are more specific than those in your textbook.)

1. The specific purpose should begin with "To inform (or persuade) my audience..."
2. The specific purpose should generally include a number of aspects, reasons, steps, etc. (between two and five). This will be the number of main points in your speech.
3. The specific purpose should state the specific topic of your speech.
4. The specific purpose, like your speech, should focus on only one main idea.

| INCORRECT | CORRECT |
| --- | --- |
| To tell about volleyball. | To inform my audience of the four (4) main skills in volleyball. |
| To inform my audience about making a memory album. | To inform my audience of the five (5) steps in making a memory album. |
| To inform my audience about the life of a person. | To inform my audience about four (4) stages in the life of Tom Osborne. |
| You should buy Levi jeans. | To persuade my audience to buy Levi jeans for three (3) reasons. |

### Guidelines for Writing a Specific Purpose and Central Idea

1. The central idea should include the number and the topic from your specific purpose.
2. The central idea should list the 2-5 specific main points you will address in your speech.
3. The central idea should match the specific purpose (both the number and the topic).

Compare the correct specific purposes (above) and the correct central ideas (below) to see how they match each other.

| INCORRECT | CORRECT |
| --- | --- |
| There are four (4) main skills in volleyball. | The four (4) main skills in volleyball are passing, setting, spiking, and serving. |
| A memory album makes a great gift. | The five (5) steps in making a memory album are collecting photos, cropping photos, organizing the page, adding stickers and paper, and writing. |
| Tom Osborne has made many important contributions during his life. | Four (4) important stages in the life of Tom Osborne are his education, his coaching, his time as a congressman, and his job as an athletic director. |
| Levi jeans are the best and so you should buy them. | Three (3) reasons you should buy Levi jeans are their superior fit, styling, and price point. |

# Chapter 3 - Getting Started

## *GUIDELINES FOR WRITING MAIN POINTS*

1. Your main points should come directly from the central idea.
2. The MAIN POINTS or MAIN IDEAS for your speech should be natural divisions, reasons, or steps to support your central idea.
3. If your specific purpose states that you will show three steps, and your central idea lists three steps, you will have three main points. Each main point will be a step.
4. You should always include at least two (2) main points, but no more than five (5) points in your speech.

Example:
**TOPIC:** German Shepherds
**GENERAL PURPOSE:** To inform
**SPECIFIC PURPOSE:** To inform my audience of _____ unique aspects of _____.

**CENTRAL IDEA:** The _____ unique aspects of _____ are
1) _____, 2) _____, and 3) _____.

MAIN POINTS:
1. German Shepherds have a unique history.
2. German Shepherds have a unique personality.
3. German Shepherds have unique jobs or roles that they perform.

Public Speaking Student Workbook

## SPECIFIC PURPOSE & CENTRAL IDEA EXERCISE

NAME: _____ CLASS TIME: _____

For each speech assignment you will be asked to choose a topic and write a specific purpose (SP) and central idea (CI) at the top of your outline. For this assignment, please choose three (3) topics for three different informative speeches. Write a specific purpose and central idea for each speech topic in the space below. (These topics are just possibilities; you will NOT be required to give speeches on the topics.)

---

Topic:

General Purpose: To inform (about a PROCESS)

Specific Purpose:

Central Idea:

---

Topic:

General Purpose: To inform (about an OBJECT or PERSON)

Specific Purpose:

Central Idea:

---

Topic:

General Purpose: To inform (about an EVENT or CONCEPT)

Specific Purpose:

Central Idea:

# Chapter 3 - Getting Started

## *SPECIFIC PURPOSE (SP) & CENTRAL IDEA (CI) EXAMPLES*
(refer back to the Guidelines on previous pages)

### Specific Purpose (SP) Format (Inform)

To inform my audience of the [*insert* number] [*insert* - steps, skills, stages] in [*insert* your full topic].

Example: To inform my audience of the three stages in the life of Abraham Lincoln.

### Central Idea (CI) Format (Inform)

The [*insert* number] [*insert* - steps, skills, stages] in [*insert* your full topic] are [*insert* what you want to inform them about]

Example: The three stages in the life of Abraham Lincoln *are* his early life, his political career, and his prosecution of the Civil War.

---

### Specific Purpose (SP) Format (Persuade)

To persuade my audience to [*insert* what you want to persuade them to do] for [*insert* number] reasons.

To persuade my audience to vote for Abe Lincoln for three reasons.

### Central Idea (CI) Format (Persuade)

[*insert* number] reasons to [*insert* what you want to persuade them to do] are [*insert* the list of reasons]

Three reasons you should vote for Abe Lincoln are he will preserve the union, he will free the slaves, and he will build the transcontinental railroad.

Public Speaking Student Workbook

## *INFORMATIVE GROUP MINI-SPEECH ASSIGNMENT*

**OBJECTIVES**

1. To practice organizing and delivering an informative speech before you deliver your first formal informative speech.
2. To meet and work with other students in the class and thus continue to promote a supportive class atmosphere.

**INSTRUCTIONS**

Form a mini-speech team of 3 to 5 students. Together choose a topic of local interest for a college audience (e.g., ethnic restaurants, night life, music, recreational areas, cultural events, historical sites, a romantic evening in our city, entertainment on a budget, recycling plans, and health or fitness clubs/facilities). Prepare an informative speech outline as a group. Divide up the speech so that each member presents some part of the speech. The time limit for the group mini-speech will be <u>3 to 5 minutes</u>, and <u>each student will be expected to speak for at least 1 minute.</u> The group outlines will be collected on the day of the mini-speeches (see mini-speech group outline on page 39).

**EXPECTATIONS & EVALUATION CRITERIA**

1. Plan and prepare the mini-speech so that each person has an equal responsibility for his/her part.

2. Each person may use one note card (5" x 8") for writing down key words to jog your memory while delivering your speech. Practice your speech with your cards several times so you know it well and know it fits the time requirements. Practice your coping strategies as you prepare your mini-speech and before you come to class.

3. Turn in one master outline for the group. Be sure to label each point of the outline with the person's name that will be responsible for delivering that part.

4. Your group will come to the front of the room on the day of the class presentations. One at a time, you will step forward and present your part. Try to make a special effort to speak conversationally and loud enough so all can hear. In addition, try to look at your audience and SMILE. Glance only occasionally at your notes.

5. You will receive ___ points for actively participating in the planning and delivering of your part in the mini-speech.

# Chapter 3 - Getting Started

## *INSTRUCTOR FEEDBACK FORM - INFORMATIVE GROUP MINI-SPEECH*

SPEAKERS: _____ DATE: _____ CLASS TIME: _____
TOPIC: _____ TIME: _____

_____ (%) POINTS EARNED

### CHECKLIST

**INTRODUCTION**
___ Gained attention ___ Related topic to audience ___ Clearly revealed topic
___ Established group credibility ___ Previewed main points in strategic order

**BODY: ORGANIZATION & DEVELOPMENT**
___ Process easy to follow ___ Main points clear ___ Used smooth transitions between points

**PRESENTATIONAL SLIDES**
___ Effective ___ Neat ___ Interesting ___ Visible for all ___ Not passed around during speech
___ Text Minimal, ___ Simple Theme, ___ Powerful Images, ___ Large Fonts, ___ Looked at Display NOT the Screen, ___ Slide Templates Attached to Outline)

**CONCLUSION**
___ Signaled the end with a signal word ___ Summarized main points ___ Motivated audience ___ Ended in an interesting way (quote, anecdote, etc.)

**DELIVERY, LANGUAGE, & IMPRESSION**
___ Eye contact for all was (circle): Excellent  Very Good  Average  Fair  Poor
___ Needed to look at all areas of the room ___ Read too much of speech
___ Looked too much at notes ___ Sporadic eye contact ___ Needed to practice more
___ Placed note card on lectern ___ Smiled occasionally at audience
___ Sounded conversational ___ Needed more enthusiasm or passion
___ Projected voice so all could hear ___ Spoke too softly ___ Spoke too loudly
___ Avoided distractions ___ Swayed body too much ___ Chewed gum
___ Gestured with pen or note card
___ Used appropriate & audience-inclusive language ___ Avoided slang or profanity
___ Sounded audience-centered ___ Interesting topic for a college audience

**OVERALL REQUIREMENTS**
___ Fulfilled time requirement ___ Each student contributed equal time & effort
___ Outline was complete ___ Points were labeled with speakers' name

**OVERALL RATING OF SPEECH** (circle): Excellent  Very Good  Good  Average  Fair  Poor

**COMMENT**

Public Speaking Student Workbook

## *INFORMATIVE GROUP MINI-SPEECH OUTLINE*

**NAMES OF GROUP MEMBERS**:
**CLASS TIME**:
**TOPIC**:
**SPECIFIC PURPOSE**:
**CENTRAL IDEA**:

**INTRODUCTION**: (NAME_____)
I. Use an attention getter:
II. Introduce topic & motivate (relate importance of topic to your audience):
III. Establish credibility:
IV. Preview main points:

**BODY**:
  I. (NAME_____)
      A.
           1.
           2.
      B.
           1.
           2.

**TRANSITION**:
  II. (NAME_____)
      A.
           1.
           2.
      B.
           1.
           2.

**TRANSITION**:
  III. (NAME_____)
      A.
           1.
           2.
      B.
           1.
           2.

**CONCLUSION**: (NAME_____)
Signal ending with a signpost:
Summarize main points:
Restate importance of topic for audience:
Add a vivid, memorable ending:

# Chapter 3 - Getting Started

NAME: _____

**OBJECTIVE:**
To create a mind map to generate ideas and organize points for your presentation

**INSTRUCTIONS:**
Mind-mapping is a visual brainstorming technique used to help you "get out" the information stored in your brain and then arrange your ideas in a reasonable order for a speech. To make a mindmap, envision a spider-like diagram and proceed with these steps:

1. Write the topic of your speech in the middle of the paper below and draw a circle around it;
2. Quickly jot down around the topic as many related ideas that flow from your mind (use single words or simple phrases), circle them and then draw lines back to the topic (like spider's legs);
3. Add more ideas related to each of the Step 2 ideas and draw lines back to those ideas: and
4. Go back and circle and number at least 3 to 5 ideas that could be main points and then circle and label ideas that could be subpoints.

Also, cross out any unneeded ideas. After you have mind-mapped your speech main points, sub-points, and sub-subpoints, you will be ready to create a speech outline.

**My Mindmap for Informative Speech I**

Public Speaking Student Workbook

*ORGANIZATIONAL PATTERNS ASSIGNMENT*

NAMES: _____

**OBJECTIVE**:
To practice creating specific purpose statements for the same topic using five different organizational patterns.

**INSTRUCTIONS**:
Choose a general topic (e.g., The Olympics). Use the space below and compose a specific purpose statement for each of the five basic organizational patterns. Use the same broad topic but narrow it as you like for each pattern.

**SUGGESTED TOPIC: Life at Our University**

1. Chronological Order (Time Pattern)
   Specific Purpose:

2. Spatial Order (Directional Pattern)
   Specific Purpose:

3. Causal Order (Cause and Effect Relationship)
   Specific Purpose:

4. Problem-Solution Order (Problem and Workable Solution)
   Specific Purpose:

5. Topical Order (e.g., Subtopics, Formats, Ways, Advantages, Reasons, etc.)
   Specific Purpose:

Chapter 3 - Getting Started

## *TEN RULES FOR OUTLINING*

1. **LABEL ALL PARTS OF YOUR OUTLINE** (i.e., Specific Purpose, Central Idea, Introduction, Body, Conclusion, and References).

2. **LABEL ALL TRANSITIONS, PREVIEWS, AND SUMMARIES**.

3. **INDENT AND USE THE STANDARD SET OF OUTLINE SYMBOLS.**
    I. <u>Main points</u> are indicated by Roman numerals (I, II, III, IV).
    II. <u>Subpoints</u> are indicated by capital letters (A, B, C).
    III. <u>Sub-subpoints</u> are indicated by Arabic numerals (1, 2, 3).
    IV. <u>Sub-sub-subpoints</u> are indicated by small letters (a, b, c). (See example below.)
   **<u>Body</u>**
    I. You need to type each MAIN POINT in a complete sentence.
        A You need to type each SUBPOINT in a complete sentence.
            1. You need to type SUB-SUBPOINTS in complete sentences.
            2. You need to type examples/quotes/statistics in your sub-subpoints
                a. no need for SUB-SUB-SUBPOINTS to be complete sentences
                b. use phrases or descriptive words
        B. You need to type at least two SUBPOINTS for each main point.
            1. You need to have at least two sub-subpoints for each subpoint.
            2. You should NOT have "1" without "2" or "a" without "b."

4. **USE COMPLETE SENTENCES FOR MAIN POINTS, SUBPOINTS and SUB-SUBPOINTS. If you use** *SUB-SUB-SUBPOINTS,* **complete sentences are not needed.** (See example.)

5. **DIVIDE AND ORDER YOUR MAIN POINTS ACCORDING TO ONE OF THE FOLLOWING FIVE ORGANIZATIONAL PATTERNS**:
    I. Chronological (Time Pattern)
    II. Spatial (Directional Pattern)
    III. Causal (Cause and Effect Pattern)
    IV. Problem-Solution
    V. Topical (Two to Five Types, Ways, Advantages, etc.)

6. **WRITE EACH MAIN POINT AND SUBPOINT SO THAT EACH CONTAINS ONLY ONE IDEA.**
   Ineffective:
   I. Since it applies more easily and costs less, latex paint is better than oil paint; it also dries faster and is not as messy.
   Effective:
   I. Latex paint is preferable to oil paint.
       A. It applies easily.
       B. It dries faster.
       C. It is not as messy.
       D. It costs less.

*Note: The number of words in a preparation outline should equal about 30% to 50% of the words in your speech. For example, since you speak about 150 words per minute, a 5-minute speech would contain 750 words. The number of words in your preparation outline would be 225 to 375.*

7. **ARRANGE SUBPOINTS TO SUPPORT YOUR MAIN POINTS**. (See ineffective example.)
    I. Proper equipment is important for playing handball.
        A. Wear good athletic shoes for maneuverability.
        B. Use padded gloves to protect your hands.
        C. Buy a handball for sufficient bounce.
        D. Have a good attitude. (This subpoint should be a separate main point.)

8. **USE AT LEAST TWO (2) MAIN POINTS, BUT DO NOT USE MORE THAN FIVE (5) MAIN POINTS**. Audiences are more likely to remember two main points with four subpoints than eight main points.

9. **HIGHLIGHT** each and every citation paragraph in your outline and **ATTACH YOUR CITING SOURCES ASSIGNMENT** for each speech (See example in Appendix).

    **Example:** According to reporter Motoko Ohtake, who wrote *Bag It, With Style* in the May 24, 2017 issue of *Newsweek*, "The problem with reusable grocery bags is that they often get left in the car or pile up at home. New ultra-compact versions, small enough to stash in a purse or clip to a key chain, are helping to solve that problem."

10. **ATTACH A LIST OF REFERENCES** (see the following page "Creating Your List of References"). List at least three (3) sources in this format:

**FOR A BOOK:**
   Author's Name (Date of Publication). *Title of book.* Place of Publication: Publisher's name.

   **Example:** Beebe, S. & Beebe, S (2014). *A concise public speaking handbook.* New York: Pearson.

**FOR A MAGAZINE OR JOURNAL ARTICLE:**
   Author's Name (Date of Publication). Name of article. *Name of Magazine,* volume #, page numbers. **Example:** Miller, K. (2018). Taming speech fright. *Lifetime Magazine, 6,* 33-38.

**For a BROCHURE or PAMPHLET from an ORGANIZATION:**
   Organization (Date of Publication). *Pamphlet title* (Brochure). Publication Place: Author or Publisher's name. **Example:** American Lung Society (2014). *How to quit smoking* (Brochure). Boston: ALA Press.

**For an INTERVIEW—in person, email or phone interview:**
   Author's Name (personal communication, date). **Example:** Henry, J. L, (personal interview, October 5, 2012).

**For an ON-LINE ELECTRONIC SOURCE** (use only reputable and recognizable academic organizations or news org. with print/ broadcast outlets):
   Author, J. (Publication date). Title of work. <u>Name of periodical</u> (On-line), pages. Available: Path [Protocol, directory, & file name] [Access date]

   **Example:** Vest, J., Cohen, W., & Tharp, M. (2010, May). Road rage. *U.S. News & World Report* (On-line), 24-30. Available: *Http://www.usnews.com/article* (2012, July 5)

# Chapter 3 - Getting Started

## *EXAMPLE OF FORMAL PREPARATION OUTLINE FORMAT*
(Use this format for outlines and label all parts.)

**Speech Title:** How to Tap Dance or Dance "the Old Soft Shoe"  **Name:** Izabella Cruz
**Organizational Pattern:** Chronological
**General Purpose:** To inform
**Specific Purpose:** To inform my audience how to tap dance in three easy steps.
**Central Idea:** The three steps involved in learning to tap dance are 1) selecting dancing attire, 2) taping your ball and heel to music and 3) practicing the basic steps of *Ball Change* and *Shuffle*.

**Introduction:** (Slide 1- Ginger Rogers & Fred Astaire, *The Old Soft Shoe*, [*Swing Time*] YouTube.
**Attention:** Have you ever heard the phrase "Give me the Old Soft Show" (popularized in vaudeville)?
**Importance:** Everyone can learn this FUN fitness tap dance that improves your rhythm and musicality.
**Credibility:** I have been tap dancing since I was four years old and now, I am a dance instructor.
**Preview:** In this speech, I will teach you how to 1) select your dancing attire, 2) tap your ball and heel to music, and 3) perform the basic *Ball Change* and *Shuffle*. **(Slide 2)**

**Body:**
I. First, you will need to choose comfortable shoes and attire.
   A. "Soft shoe" Is a "relaxed, graceful dance done in any flat soft-soled shoes" and is a form of tap dance (author) Rusty Frank (Credibility) in Encyclopedia Britannica (Source) in 2016 (Date).
     1. Choose flat dress shoes with good soles. **(Slide 3)**
     2. Make sure the shoes do not have a ridge on the bottom.
   B. Tap shoes have metal plates at the toe and shoes with decent ones costing $75.00 and up.
     1. Choose ones that you feel have good comfort, fit and floor sound. **(refer to Slide 3)**
     2. Look for three screws in each metal plate on the toe and heel.
   C. Select comfortable workout clothes, which are important for all exercise and practice.
(**Transition:** Now that I have informed you about dance shoes and attire, it's time to tap the *Ball Heel*.

II. The second step in learning to tap dance is to practice the *Ball Heel* with music. **(Slide 4)**
   A. Stand with bent knees, body weight on top of your feet and with hands on your hips.
     1. Extend one foot to the front and start with the ball tap.
     2. Lift the leg and tap with the ball of your foot (listen for the click); lower your heel sharply and repeat.
   B. Practice *Ball Heel* taping with both feet to music.
     1. Listen to the music and try to tap with the beat of the music.
     2. Try songs such as *Shim Sham* by Peggy Lee or *Counting the Stars* by OneRepublic.
(**Transition:** After you have learned to tap the *Ball Heel* to music, it is time to learn two easy steps.)

III. The third step is to learn and practice the basic *Ball Change* and *Shuffle*. **(Slide 5)**
   A. For the *Ball Change*, lift one foot, balancing on the other, step down and shift your weight.
     1. Rock back and forth between feet (if you step forward, it becomes a *Step Ball Change*).
     2. Your heels will stay in the air so that only the balls of your feet touch the ground.
   B. For the *Shuffle*, stand on the left foot, bend your right leg behind you and swing it forward.
     1. Tap the ball of the right foot on the floor, swing it back and repeat.
     2. Stomp it back on the floor next to your left foot. Repeat with other foot.

**Conclusion:**
**Signpost and Summary:** In conclusion, you have now learned the three basic steps to tap dancing:1) select attire, 2) tap the *Ball Heel* to music, and perform the *Ball Change* and *Shuffle* steps. **(Slide 6)**
**Importance:** You can enjoy this FUN fitness dance and improve your rhythm and musicality.
**Memorable Ending:** Picture yourself dancing like this (I will tap dance for a few seconds).
**References:** Frank, R. (2016) Tap dance. In *Encyclopedia Britannica* (Mobile application software). **Retrieved from https://www.britannica.com/art/tap-dace#ref205308.**Rogers & Astaire (1936). The Old Soft Shoe [Swing Time]. **Retrieved from https://www.youtube.com/watch?v= mxPgplMujzQ**

*Example of A Delivery Outline*
*5" X 8" Speaker's Card*
*"How to Tap Dance" Outline*

**Remember Eye Contact!!**
**INTRO (Slide 1-** Video: *The Old Soft Shoe* with Ginger Rogers and Fred Astaire in 1936 [*Swing Time*]]

1. Heard: **"Give me the Old Soft Show"** – [vaudeville)?
2. **FUN fitness** tap dance
3. Tap **dancing since 4 and now instructor.**
4. **1) Dancing attire, 2) tap** *Ball and Heel* to music, **and 3)** *Ball Change* **and** *Shuffle*.

**SMILE!!!**
BODY
I. **First, choose comfortable** shoes and attire.**(Slide 2)**

   A. "Soft shoe" Is a "relaxed, graceful dance done in any flat soft-soled shoes" and is a form of tap dance according to Rusty Frank in *Encyclopedia Britannica*.

   **Choose flat dress** shoes. **(Slide 3)**
   **No ridge** on bottom. OR

   B. Tap shoes -**metal plates** - $75.00 and up.
   **Comfort, fit and sound. (refer to Slide 3)**
   **Three screws** - metal plates (**show tap shoes**)

   C. **Select comfortable** workout attire clothes

(**Transition**: Now that I…s time to tap the *Ball Heel*.

II. **The second step -** *Ball Heel* **with music. (Slide 4)**
   A. **Bent knees, body** weight - hands on hips.
   B. **Practice** *Ball Heel* **to music. (Play Refer to Slide 4)**
*Shim Sham* by Peggy Lee or *Counting the Stars* by OneRepublic.

(**Transition**: After you have *Ball Heel* to music… two easy steps.)

III. The **third step -** *Ball Change* **and** *Shuffle*. **(Slide 5)**
   *Ball Change*, lift, balance, shift weight and ROCK **(SHOW)**
   *Shuffle,* stand, swing, tap, swing it back, Repeat. **(SHOW)**

CONCLUSION
IN CONCLUSION, Three basic steps: (SLIDE 6)
**Enjoy FUN fitness dance -** rhythm and musicality.
**Picture yourself** dancing like this **(SHOW)**.

# Chapter 3 - Getting Started
## *CITING YOUR SOURCES & MAKING A REFERENCE LIST*

In all your speeches, you must <u>use and cite at least 5 pieces of supporting material from 3 different types of sources</u> (e.g., book, magazine, journal, newspaper, Internet website, interview). Please list all sources in your <u>References List</u>. Use the following format in your speech and on your outline and note cards. To cite your sources, cover these four parts: 1) **author,** 2) **author's credibility**, 3) **source**, and 4) **date**. For example, you might say:

> In a *Canadian Geographic* article entitled *Wave Warning* **(Source)** written by geologist **(Credibility),** Sarah Ephron, **(Author)** in October 2018 **(Date):** "When a tsunami warning is sounded at least one half-hour in advance, most lives have been saved."

> According to a feature article called, *If you Think Gas is High, Try Europe* written by Bruce Crumley **(Author)** in the May 28, 2018 **(date)** issue of Time Magazine, **(source)**, the Europeans are paying more than double what Americans pay for gas. Crumley reported, "As American drivers groan over prices nearing $4 a gallon, the French are paying $8.67 for a gallon of *super*."

A **Reference List** includes only the sources you refer to in your speech. Type *Reference List* at the end of your outline and list all sources in alphabetical order. Use APA style and label your sources by type. See examples below for formatting and citing sources on your outline.

## <u>APA Reference List Examples</u>

**Books**
   Author, I. (Publication Date). <u>The Title of the Book.</u> Publication Place (City): Publisher.
   *Examples – One Author and Two or More Authors*
   Lucas, S. (2019). *The art of public speaking.* New York: McGraw-Hill Education.
   Ford, R., & Audi. J. (2019). *Building an electric car.* Boston: Allen Publishing.

**<u>Magazines, Newspapers, or Journals</u>**
   Author, I. (Publication Date). Title of article. <u>Magazine,</u> <u>volume number</u>, page numbers.
   *Example – Magazine, Journal Article, or Newspaper Article*
   Miller, K. (2016, May 25). Taming speech anxiety. *Lifetime Magazine,* <u>6</u>, 33-38.

**<u>Brochures, Pamphlets, Video, Film, or Television</u>**
   Organization. (Publication Date). *Title of brochure or video.* Publication Place: Publisher.
   *Examples – Brochure, Video, and Television*
   American Lung Assoc. (2015). *How to quit smoking.* (Brochure). Omaha: Midwest Press.
   Lucas, J. (Producer) (2017). Star Wars [film]. Hollywood: Paramount.
   Fox, N. (Producer) (2020). Tom Cruise talks tough. Sixty Minutes. New York: ABCNY.

**<u>On-Line Electronic Sources</u>** (**Note: Acceptable on-line sources include only reputable and recognizable news or academic organizations with print or broadcast outlets.)
   Author, I. (Publication Date or Recent Update). Title. *Name of Periodical* (On-line), pages.

   Available (yes): Path (Protocol, directory, & file name) (Access Date).
   *Example – Magazine Article on the Internet*
   Vest, J., Cohen, W., & Tharp, M. (2019, May). Road rage. *U.S. News & World Report* (Online), 24-30. Available: http://www.usnews.com/article J02 (2020 July 5).

**<u>Interviews – in person, email or phone interview</u>**
   *Example – Interview in Person*   Author, I. (personal communication type, date)
   (Henry, J. L. (personal interview, October 5, 2021).

Public Speaking Student Workbook

## *SPEECH INTRODUCTION EXERCISE*

**NAMES:** _____

**OBJECTIVE:**
To create a captivating and effective introduction for an informative speech.

**INSTRUCTIONS:**
Form a team of 2 to 3 students. Choose an informative speech topic from the list provided below. Narrow the topic and write a specific purpose and central idea. Then write an introduction that includes these four (4) objectives:

1. Get the attention and interest of your audience for the topic.

2. Introduce the topic and motivate your audience to listen (relate the importance of the topic to your audience).

3. Establish speaker credibility and good will.

4. Preview the body of the speech (mention each main point in strategic order).

**EXPECTATIONS:**

1. Work together on each objective in the introduction. All members of the team are expected to actively participate.

2. Use the space provided below to write your draft.

3. Suggested topics include: Antiques, Baseball Card Collections, Community Playhouse, Computer Games, Concerts, Dancing, Gourmet Cooking, Swimming, Martial Arts, Mountain Climbing, Olympics, Parasailing, Photography, Quilting, Star Trek, Sun Tanning, or Weight Lifting.

---

**TOPIC:**

**SPECIFIC PURPOSE:**

**CENTRAL IDEA:**

**THE INTRODUCTION:**

# Chapter 3 - Getting Started
## *INTRODUCING THE SPEAKER*

**For the Introducer Worksheet, see the next page.**

**OBJECTIVES**:
1. To introduce the speaker and set the mood for the presentation.
2. To assist the speaker and help him/her feel at ease.

**INSTRUCTIONS**:

Your role as an introducer is to help the speaker feel at ease and assist him/her in any way possible directly before and after the speech. Plan to introduce the speaker by giving the speaker's name plus two pieces of information about the speaker. (You will need to briefly talk to each speaker before you plan the introductions.) You will want to mention the speaker's topic, but do not go into any detail about it or give your opinion. The speaker will still need to establish his/her own credibility in the speech. You may use a note card, but do not read your introductions. Examples of appropriate introductions include:

*Our next speaker is Jane Jones. Jane has been taking pictures all her life and has just finished her second course in photojournalism. "Today, she will speak to us on How to Take the Best Selfies." Let's welcome Jane (CLAP).*

*I would like to introduce to you Maggie Smith. You already know that Maggie is a sophomore, majoring in political science, but did you know that she worked last summer for our State Legislator, Sam Chambers? Maggie is going to inform us "How a Bill Becomes a Law" (CLAP).*

*Please welcome Greg Walton. Originally from Iowa City, Greg just returned from Afghanistan. He has been in many stressful situations, so the topic of his speech is "Overcoming Stress" (CLAP).*

**REQUIREMENTS AND EVALUATION CRITERIA**:
1. Talk to your speaker to get the title of the speech and two pieces of information about the speech or speaker. Also, check to see if you can assist with visual aids, lighting, etc.

2. As the introducer, you walk to the front of the classroom, make your introduction, and stand there until the speaker moves to his/her place near or behind the lectern. Then take your seat near the front of the room. At the end of the speech, stand in the front again, and ask the audience for questions. Call on a few people. The question-and-answer time should last about one minute. (Look for your instructor's signal.) Thank the speaker, and again ask for applause. After the speaker is seated, introduce the next speaker. (Be prepared to ask a question or fill the time, if no one volunteers a question.)

3. You will receive ___ points for introducing the speakers as described above.

Public Speaking Student Workbook
*INTRODUCING THE SPEAKER WORKSHEET*

INTRODUCER: _____ DATE: _____
SPEAKERS:_____
(Turn in at the end of the day you introduce)

**Prepared to introduce and in class on time** _____

**Showed enthusiasm in giving introductions** _____

**Introduced speaker by:**
- waiting until speaker is ready before starting
- giving at least two pieces of information and then giving name at the end (e.g., "Our first speaker………please welcome "name")
- assisting the speaker, if needed (ask speaker for what assistance is needed, if any) _____

**Initiated applause for speaker twice**-- at the end of introduction and at the end of the question-answer time _____

**Conducted a question-answer time at the end of the speech:**
- included 2 to 3 questions
- covered about 1 minute of time
- prepared questions, if needed, to get things started) _____

See Workbook p. 48 for more details

\* \* \* \* \* \*
**Speakers**

**1st speaker:**


**2nd speaker:**


**3rd speaker:**


**4th speaker:**

# 4

# Informative Speaking

**Speech Assignments**

**Speech Topic & Research Reports,**

**Self-Evaluations,**

**Instructor Evaluations,**

**Audience Analysis Exercise**

**Language Assignment**

Public Speaking Student Workbook

# *INFORMATIVE SPEECH ASSIGNMENT #1 – THE PROCESS SPEECH*

**SPEECH DUE DATE:**
**OUTLINE DUE DATE:**
**TIME LIMIT: 3 to 5 Minutes**

## OBJECTIVES
1. To increase the audience's knowledge or understanding of a specific process so that they are enabled to describe, explain, or perform the process.
2. To demonstrate using <u>presentational software</u> and VISUAL AIDS <u>how a process is completed</u> or <u>how it works.</u>

## INSTRUCTIONS
Your first formal speech is designed to help you develop and practice public speaking skills. Choose a topic that you know a lot about, have enthusiasm for, and can make interesting to a college audience (both men and women). Create a presentation slideshow that includes six slides and clarifies your process (see Tips on Creating Presentational Slides). Also, bring at least visual aid that shows the procedure. **Do NOT bring any of the following items to class:** <u>illegal substances, harmful or hazardous materials, alcohol, pornography, animals, insects, guns, knives or weapons of any kind, needles, syringes or drug paraphernalia</u>. These items are NOT allowed on state property because they could harm others. **In addition, you cannot perform any medical or other process** (e.g., CPR, Heimlich maneuver, etc.) **on another person in your class**. Examples of topics include: How to Drive a Golf Ball, How to Buy a Good Pair of Athletic Shoes, How a Guitar Produces Music, How a Jet Engine Works, How to Take Pictures Like a Professional Photographer, How to Repair a Leaky Faucet.

## REQUIREMENTS AND EVALUATION CRITERIA
1. Your slide show and visual aid must be an integral part of your speech. Use ONLY six to eight slides and do NOT read from the screen. Please email your slide show to your instructor before you speak.
2. Your speech should be effectively organized, outlined, introduced, and concluded.
3. Your preparation outline must be prepared and <u>typed</u> following formal outline format. Your preparation outline is due one class period before all speeches are scheduled. Your speaking note card is due immediately following your speech.
4. Your speech must be delivered extemporaneously from notes. Do NOT prepare a speech manuscript; do NOT memorize a manuscript. Please use only ___ note card(s) (5" x 8") for your speaking notes.
5. Practice all your coping strategies as you prepare your speech. Practice your speech several times and <u>TIME your speech</u>!
6. After class, view your recorded presentation and write a self-evaluation of your presentation. (Ask the Speech Center instructor to stamp your form.) Your self-evaluation is due the class period after the last round of informative speeches.
7. This assignment is worth a possible <u>100 points</u>. Evaluation criteria include: Introduction, Organization & Use of Transitions, Content Development, Use of Visual Aids, Conclusion, Extemporaneous & Conversational Delivery, and Overall – Time Limit, Audience-centeredness, and Outlines.

# Chapter 4 - Informative Speaking

## *TIPS FOR USING VISUAL AIDS*

1. Include a slide show of six to eight slides as one of the visual aids for your speech.

2. Follow the *Presentational Slides Assignment & Guidelines* on Workbook page 54 and submit your slide show with your outline. Then email your slide show to your instructor before your speech.

**For any additional Visual aids use the following guidelines:**

3. Do NOT PASS your visual aid around the classroom BEFORE or DURING your speech. If you want to pass around treats related to the topic of your speech, a recipe, a list of addresses, etc., do it quickly at the END of your speech.

4. When using slides, list the steps, point to each step and present one at a time.

5. Talk to your audience, NOT the visual aid.

6. Do NOT block the view of your visual aid by standing in front of it. Do NOT turn your back on your audience.

7. Do NOT just show your visual aid. You must use it and talk about it. Do NOT show your visual aid until you are ready to refer to it. Display it long enough so all can see it.

8. If you are showing a process, plan to bring a visual that will take us through each step (e.g., baking, ceramics, changing oil, etc.).

9. Plan to bring a visual aid to class on the day of your presentation. If you are using yourself as a visual aid, then you should dress appropriately for your topic and you should demonstrate something (e.g., wear a basketball uniform to demonstrate free throws; wear workout clothes to demonstrate CrossFit). <u>Unless your hat is part of your visual aid, please remove it while delivering your speech.</u>

**LIST OF ITEMS DUE FOR INFORMATIVE SPEECH #1**
_ Completed Speech #1 Checklist (p. 56)
_ Typed Preparation Outline
_ Slides Template (see Workbook Appendix) and *Presentational Slides Guidelines* on the next two pages
_ Typed References — including who helped you learn the activity or who coached you
_ Slides Emailed to YOUR Instructor before the day of your speech
_ Speaking Card(s)

**Bring your workbook to class for these two forms**
_ Instructor's evaluation form
_ Peer feedback forms

Public Speaking Student Workbook

## TOPIC, SPECIFIC PURPOSE, AND CENTRAL IDEA REPORT #1
## INFORMATIVE SPEECH #1 – A PROCESS SPEECH

Name:_____  Class Time: _____

Topic:

**Rationale** (Why did you choose this topic and these points?):

**General Purpose**: TO INFORM

**Specific Purpose**:

**Central Idea**:

**Organizational Pattern**:

<u>**Ideas for Main Points**</u> (include at least three points written in complete sentences):

I.

II.

III.

IV.

V.


**Slide show and Visual Aid Ideas** (use the templates in the Workbook Appendix, p. 226).


**Ideas for the Introduction or Conclusion**:

Chapter 4 - Informative Speaking

## *PRESENTATIONAL SLIDES ASSIGNMENT & GUIDELINES*

**OBJECTIVE: To create SIX to EIGHT presentational slides, using** *PowerPoint, Canva, Keynote or Google Slides* **to use as visual aids to enhance your speech.**

**Follow these guidelines**: Then create 1) a title slide, 2) an attention slide, 3) a preview slide, 4-6) ONE slide for each of your main point slides, 7) a conclusion summary slide, and 8) a memorable ending slide. Plan to make them easy to read and DO NOT read from them during your speech. Plan using the slide templates, located in the appendix of this workbook.

1. *Keep text to a minimum.* Use only concise phrases or key words. Think in terms of a billboard that people see and comprehend in seconds. You can elaborate on the words during your speech. Too much information on a slide will force your audience to read, which keeps them from listening to you. **RULE:** Use few words and make only ONE point per slide.

2. *Choose a simple theme.* You are the star, not the slides, so use a simple background slide with plenty of white space. Try not use a pre-packaged cookie-cutter slide template. **RULE:** Your slide should look uncluttered and be easy to see — no logos needed.

3. *Use color to maximize visibility.* Choose a sharp contrast between the color of the slide background and the color of the fonts (e.g., use a dark background with light text or vice versa). **RULE:** Consider what will display best, depending on the light in the room.

4. *Use simple images.* Whenever possible, use a picture or image to illustrate or make your point. **RULE:** Do not use an image simply to decorate your slide, but instead, let it represent or powerfully make your point.

5. *Be wise about fonts and effects.* Use common fonts like Arial, Verdana, or Tahoma, between 36 to 44-point type for titles, and 28 to 32-point type for subtitles or text, NO SMALLER. Use **Sans Serif** fonts (e.g., Arial, Century Gothic, Helvetica, Tahoma, Calibri, Lucida Sans or Verdana) **for titles** and **Serif** fonts (e.g., letters with tails — Times Roman, Bookman, Century, Garamond, Lucida) **for subtitles** to give contrast. **RULE:** Do not use ALL CAPS to emphasize a word (its looks like you are shouting), be careful with **BOLD type or italics** because both are hard to distinguish when projected and **use sound effects and unusual transitions sparingly**.

6. *Illustrate numerical data.* Instead of presenting complex data in a tabular format, convert the data into a clear, well-designed bar, pie or line graphs. **RULE:** Use appropriate charts or graphs that can easily convey a numerical message without forcing the audience to analyze the data.

7. *Add citations.* Briefly document images and all supporting material on your slides.

8. *Practice with your slides.* Your visuals should enhance your presentation. **RULE:** Always establish eye contact with your audience and look ONLY at the computer display; **DO NOT** look at your slides on the projector screen.

*Plan your slides following these guidelines and use* **the templates in the Workbook Appendix, p. 226**. Submit the slide templates with your outline and email your instructor your slideshow so it will be available on the day you speak.

Public Speaking Student Workbook

## *INSTRUCTOR EVALUATION FORM – INFORMATIVE SPEECH #1*

_____TOTAL PERCENTAGE (%) POINTS     _____GRADE

NAME:_____ DATE: _____
TOPIC:_____ TIME: _____

KEY   EXCELLENT (5 ++)   GOOD (4 +)   FAIR (3 √)   WEAK (1 or 2 √--)   OMITTED (O)

### SPEECH OUTLINE & PREPARATION - 15 (%) POINTS
__Preparation Outline completed (__sections labeled, __indented, __full sentences, __transitions, __references)
__Speaking Outline completed (__large cards, __dark print, __brief notes, __legible, large print)
__Chose appropriate topic, clear process – remained informative, & adapted it to audience

### INTRODUCTION - 15 (%) POINTS
__Gained interest of audience (__captured attention for topic, __motivated audience to listen)
__Established your credibility (__why & __how you know about topic)
__Previewed main points in strategic order (__clear central idea) & fully introduced topic

### BODY = ORGANIZATION, DEVELOPMENT, & TRANSITIONS - 25 (%) POINTS
__Main points easily identified
__Effective organizational pattern (__ideas arranged logically) & manageable number of main points
__Each main point developed with sufficient details (points were not __too long or __too brief)
__Clear explanation of process or activities (__points were easy to follow)
__Smooth connectives between main points (__used signal words, __used transitions)

### USE OF PRESENTATIONAL SOFTWARE & VISUAL AIDS - 10 (%) POINTS
__Effective use of visual aids (__visible, __impacting, __ timing, __looked at audience NOT the visual aid)
__Presentational Slides (__text minimal, __simple theme, __powerful images, __large fonts, __looked at display NOT the screen, __slide templates attached to outline)

### PRESENTATION & DELIVERY - 20 (%) POINTS
__Strong eye contact (__looked at all areas of the room, __looked only occasionally at notes, __eye contact was sustained throughout speech, __preparation & practice were evident)
__Effective use of voice (__sounded conversational, __used vocal variety to eliminate a monotonous voice, __used appropriate vocal rate – not too fast or too slow, __projected voice so all could hear, __paused effectively with few uhms)
__Expressive & used appropriate, audience-inclusive language (__sounded sincere, enthusiastic or passionate, __used language free of slang and profanity)
__Effective facial expression, gestures, & animation (__used appropriate movement – not stiff or pacing, __avoided distractions – little or no swaying, no gum chewing, __used natural hand gestures)

### CONCLUSION & TIMING - 15 (%) POINTS
__Signaled ending (__used a signal word) & summarized main points (__restated each main point)
__Used vivid, interesting ending (__used quote or anecdote to make conclusion memorable)
__Adherence to time limit (__filled time requirement – not too short or too long)
____Time of Speech     ____Outline Handed in on Time     ____Remained Informative
**COMMENTS:**

# Chapter 4 - Informative Speaking
## *INFORMATIVE SPEECH #1 — SPEAKER CHECKLIST*

Please use this checklist to prepare your first speech. It will help you get the best grade possible. When you turn in your outline, please include this completed checklist with it.

### ✓ Preparation Outline

- Clear Specific Purpose.
- Clear Central Idea
- Typed formal outline format using the ten rules for outlining—see Workbook p. 42.
    - Labeled all parts of outline.
    - Used complete sentences throughout.
    - Used Roman numerals, letters, and numbers.
    - Highlighted supporting material
- Attached slide templates to outline in the appendix.

### ✓ Introduction

- Attention: In the introduction, stimulate your audience's interest in the topic and explain how it will help them. (Please do not begin: "Today I am going to tell you ….")
- Credibility: State how you know about the topic and why you are interested in it.
- Preview: Express the main points in your speech.

### ✓ Speech Body

- Speech Development: Use at least 2 main points with sub-points A and B and sub-sub-points 1 and 2 for each point. This is the minimal requirement.
- Transition: Use a full connective between each main point and the next main point.
- Process: The speech demonstrates a clear process.
- Presentational Slides: Followed assignment guidelines & used slides effectively.

### ✓ Conclusion

- Sign post: Signal ending (e.g., *in review, in conclusion, in summary, as we end*).
- Summary: Summarize all main points in your speech.
- Importance to Audience: State how your information presented is helpful or important for your audience.
- Memorable Ending: Use a statistic, illustration, example, quotation, etc.

### ✓ Note Cards

- Note cards are completed and numbered with main sections clearly labeled.
    - Brief notes for each point.
    - Lettering is large and easy to read.

### ✓ Speech Practice

- I practiced the speech to verify it falls within the time limit.
- I practiced using brief notes for each point.
- I practiced with my visual aids and slides.

Public Speaking Student Workbook

## *SELF-EVALUATION FORM for INFORMATIVE SPEECH #1*

NAME:_____ CLASS TIME: _____
TOPIC: _____ DATE: _____

**OBJECTIVES**:
1. To critically evaluate your own presentation.
2. To set goals to work on for your next speech in order to improve your presentation.

**INSTRUCTIONS**:
View your recording one or more times. Use this evaluation form to analyze and evaluate the strengths and areas for improvement in your presentation.

1. **INTRODUCTION** (Gained Attention, Motivated Audience to Listen, Clearly Introduced Topic, Established Credibility, Previewed Main Points):

   Strengths:

   Areas for Improvement:

2. **BODY** (Manageable Number of Main Points, Effective Organizational Pattern, Smooth Transitions, Points Easily Identified, Easy to Follow):

   Strengths:

   Areas for Improvement:

3. **USE OF SLIDES & VISUAL AIDS** (Slides Used Minimal Text, a Simple Theme, Powerful Images, Large Fonts; You Looked at Display NOT the Screen AND All Visual Aids Were an Integral Part of Speech, Neat, Impactful, Clearly Visible by All & Used Effectively):

   Strengths:

   Areas for Improvement:

4. **DELIVERY & EXPRESSION** (Eye Contact, Conversational Delivery, Vocal Variety, Pauses (few uhms), Volume, Rate, Gestures, Enthusiasm, Appropriate Language):

   Strengths:

   Areas for Improvement:

5. **CONCLUSION** (Signaled Ending, Summarized Main Points, Restated Importance of Topic to Audience, Used Vivid & Memorable Ending):

   Strengths:

   Areas for Improvement:

## OVERALL EVALUATION

6. Were you Audience-Centered and Sincere? Explain.

7. Were you satisfied or happy with your speech overall? Explain.

8. What would you do differently if you could give your speech again?

9. Describe ONE OR TWO goals you will work on to improve your next speech.

Public Speaking Student Workbook

## IN-CLASS AUDIENCE ANALYSIS QUESTIONNAIRE ACTIVITY

NAME: _____

### OBJECTIVES
1. To practice using an audience analysis questionnaire.
2. To meet and work with other students in the class and thus continue to promote a supportive class atmosphere.

### INSTRUCTIONS
1. Form a team of 4 students. Together, complete the questionnaire (next page) on the topic *Drinking Water for your Health*.

2. Collect the questionnaires tally the responses below and analyze the knowledge and attitude your audience has about your topic.

3. Create an introduction for a speech. Use statistics or quotations from your tally to write a citation paragraph to create interest and relate to your audience's knowledge and attitudes.

### AUDIENCE ANALYSIS QUESTIONNAIRE TALLY
Record your audience's responses on a tally sheet. Then summarize your audience's interest in, knowledge of, and attitude toward the topic in the space below.

#### Fixed-Alternative Questions
1) Summary of answers and how you will adapt to your audience.


2) Summary of answers and how you will adapt to your audience.


#### Scale Questions
3) Summary of answers and how you will adapt to your audience.


4) Summary of answers and how you will adapt to your audience.


#### Open-Ended Questions
5) Summary of answers and how you will adapt to your audience.


6) Summary of answers and how you will adapt to your audience.


**Introduction:** Write out a citation paragraph for a statistic, testimony, or example from the survey that you could use in a speech introduction.

Chapter 4 - Informative Speaking

## SAMPLE AUDIENCE ANALYSIS SURVEY
### 💧💧 Drinking Water Survey 💧💧

## Fixed Alternative Questions

1. Do you like to drink water?

    Yes_____ No_____

2. Do you use any sort of purified water (bottled water, water purifier, etc.) instead of tap water?

    Yes_____ No_____ Only Occasionally_____

## Scale Questions

3. How many glasses of water do you drink in an average day?

| One | Two | Three | Four | Five | Six | Seven | Eight | Nine | Ten |
|---|---|---|---|---|---|---|---|---|---|

4. I prefer to drink other beverages (e.g., pop, juice, coffee, etc.) instead of water.

| Strongly Agree | Agree | Neutral | Disagree | Strongly Disagree |
|---|---|---|---|---|

## Open-ended Questions

5. When you choose to drink beverages other than water, why do you choose them?

6. What motivates you to drink water when you do?

**For the Activity and Questionnaire Instructions—See the previous page.

Public Speaking Student Workbook

## ANALYZING & USING SUPPORTING MATERIAL

NAME: _____

**OBJECTIVE:**
To analyze how supporting material is used in magazine or newspaper articles.

**INSTRUCTIONS**
Choose a newspaper or magazine article. Circle as many types of supporting material as you can find in the article. Next, under the appropriate type of supporting material (listed below), record one sentence of the material and the source (note the way it was cited). **Staple your article to this page.**

Article Title: _____ Source: _____ Date: _____

### TYPES OF SUPPORTING MATERIAL

1. **Illustrations or Examples**
    a. Brief

    Source Cited:

    b. Extended

    Source Cited:

    c. Hypothetical

    Source Cited:

2. **Statistics**
    a. Numbers or Percentages

    Source Cited:

    b. Dates

    Source Cited:

3. **Testimony (quotations or paraphrase)**
    a. Lay (or Peer)

    Source Cited:

    b. Expert

    Source Cited:

Chapter 4 - Informative Speaking

## *INFORMATIVE SPEECH #2 — SPEAKER CHECKLIST*

Please use this checklist to prepare your first speech. It will help you get the best grade possible. When you turn in your outline, please include this completed checklist with it.

**Preparation Outline**

- Clear Specific Purpose and Central Idea
- Typed formal outline format using the ten rules for outlining—see Workbook p. 42
  - Labeled all parts of outline, used complete sentences, and used Roman numerals, letters, and numbers.
  - Highlighted citation paragraphs and language device—simile, metaphor, repetition, parallelism, antithesis, or alliteration).
  - List of References and Slide Templates (if slides used) are attached
- Audience Analysis questionnaire, tally, with summary on p. 70 attached

**Introduction**

- Attention: In the introduction, stimulate your audience's interest in the topic and explain how it will help them. (Please do not begin: "Today I am going to tell you ….")
- Credibility: State how you know about the topic and why you are interested in it.
- Preview: Express the main points in your speech.

**Speech Body Development and Supporting Material**

- Speech Development: Use at least 2 main points with sub-points *A* and *B* and sub-sub-points *1* and *2* for each point. This is the minimal requirement.
- Used at least five pieces of supporting material.
  - At least one statistic is cited.
  - At least one testimony/opinion is cited.
  - At least one example is cited.
- At least three different types of sources are cited. Wikipedia is NOT a source.
- All five citation paragraphs are complete with source, author, credibility, and date.
- Used a quotation or statistic from your audience analysis.
- References are in APA format and are attached to the outline.

**Conclusion**

- Sign post: Signal ending (e.g., use words such as, *in review, in conclusion,* etc.)
- Summary: Summarize all main points in your speech.
- Importance to Audience: State how your information is helpful for your audience.
- Memorable Ending: Use a statistic, illustration, example, quotation, etc.

**Note Cards & Speech Practice**

- Note cards are completed—brief notes, large lettering, labeled, and numbered.
- I practiced the speech to verify it falls within the time limit.
- I practiced using the note cards.
- I practiced with my visual aids and slides.

Public Speaking Student Workbook

*INFORMATIVE SPEECH ASSIGNMENT #2*
**200 POINTS**

**SPEECH DUE DATE:**
**OUTLINE DUE DATE:**
**TIME LIMIT: 4 to 6 Minutes**

**OBJECTIVES**:
1. To increase the audience's understanding and knowledge of a particular concept, object, person, or event.
2. To use a variety of supporting materials (e.g., quotations, examples, statistics) from a variety of sources in order to add depth to your speech, to add evidence in support of your ideas, and to maintain your audience's interest in the topic.
3. To use descriptive language and a stylistic device, effective delivery techniques, and self-evaluation in order to increase speaker effectiveness.

**INSTRUCTIONS**:
Your second formal informative speech is designed to help you further develop speech making skills. You may give your speech on a concept, an object/ person, or an event, but not on a process because that was the requirement for your first informative speech. A variety of topics would be appropriate. For example, you might present a biographical sketch on Winston Churchill or you might research and explain the history and purpose of Daylight Savings Time, the causes and treatments of Lupus, the significance of the Battle of Gettysburg, or the causes of the landslide election of 1932. Some topics might lend themselves to persuasive as well as informative presentations. However, you should stick to informing your audience for this speech. (Do NOT tell the audience what they should do or believe or that something is a problem or is beneficial.) If you use visual aids, please follow the visual aid assignment requirements AND guidelines on p. 54 in this workbook.

**REQUIREMENTS AND EVALUATION CRITERIA**:
1. Your speech should be effectively organized, outlined, introduced, and concluded as you did for the last speech.

2. Your main points should be clearly supported by at least a total of FIVE (5) PIECES of supporting material (*with highlighted citation paragraphs*) from at least three different types of sources. Your examples, statistics, and quotations must be cited in 1) Your Speech, 2) Your Speech Outline, and 3) Your References. You must include a minimum of THREE DIFFERENT TYPES of sources in your list of references (e.g., book, newspaper, magazine, website, etc.) and use proper APA Style for each citation (see Workbook p. 43).

3. You should adapt your speech to your audience based upon the results of your audience analysis questionnaire. Please administer an audience analysis survey (including two (2) fixed-alternative questions, two (2) scale questions, and two (2) open-ended questions) to your class when assigned. Attach to your outline a copy of your survey with a tally of your results and a summary for each question (see p. 70) describing what you learned and how you will adapt to your audience.

## Chapter 4 - Informative Speaking

4. You will need to use at least one stylistic language device to add imagery or cadence to your speech (e.g., simile, metaphor, repetition, parallelism, antithesis, or alliteration).

5. Your preparation outline (including the references) must be prepared and TYPED following formal outline format. Your preparation outline is due one class period before all speeches are scheduled. Your speaking note cards are due immediately following your presentation.

6. Your speech must be delivered extemporaneously from notes. Do NOT prepare a speech manuscript; do NOT memorize a manuscript. Please use only 3 note cards (5" x 8") for your speaking notes. Practice your speech several times before the day of your presentation.

7. If you use visual aids, please follow the presentational slides guidelines on Workbook p. 54 and submit your templates and slide show to your instructor in advance.

8. After class, you will view your recorded speech and do a self-evaluation of your presentation. (Ask the Speech Center instructor to stamp your form.) <u>Your self-evaluation is due the class period after the last round of informative speeches</u>.

9. This assignment is worth a possible ___ points. Evaluation criteria include: Introduction, Organization & Use of Transitions, Content Development, Use of Supporting Material & Visual Aids, Use of Language, Conclusion, Delivery, and Overall — Time Limit, Audience-Centeredness, Audience-Analysis, Outlines.

**LIST OF ITEMS DUE FOR INFORMATIVE SPEECH #2**
_ Completed Informative Speech #2 Checklist on p. 62
_ Typed Preparation Outline – with highlighted citation paragraphs
_ Typed References
_ Audience Analysis Questionnaire with Tally of Your Audience Responses (use p. 70)
_ Speaking Card(s)
_ Completed Library Assignment
_ Completed Citing Sources Assignment (p. 68)
_ Slides Template, if slides are used – follow the guidelines from Workbook p. 54, submit
   templates with your outline and then email your slideshow to your instructor in advance.

  _ **Bring your workbook to class for these two forms**
     _ Instructor's evaluation form
     _ Peer feedback form

**LIBRARY ASSIGNMENT**
The Library Assignment will help you find sources for supporting material and citations for your speech. You will need to attach it to your preparation outline. Please download the required assignment as assigned by your instructor.

Public Speaking Student Workbook

## TOPIC, SPECIFIC PURPOSE, CENTRAL IDEA, & RESEARCH REPORT
## INFORMATIVE SPEECH #2

NAME_____ CLASS TIME_____

**MY PERSONAL GOAL FOR THIS SPEECH** (based upon your self-evaluation of your last speech, please explain your new goals--e.g., increase eye contact, use more conversational delivery):

**Topic**:

**Rationale** (Why did you choose this topic?):

**General Purpose**: To inform (about a concept, object/ person, or event — **Circle one**).

**Specific Purpose**:

**Central Idea**:

**Organizational Pattern:**

**Ideas for Main Points (include at least three points written in complete sentences):**

I.

II.

III.

IV.

V.

**Ideas for Optional Slides or Visual Aid:**

**Ideas for the Introduction or Conclusion:**

# Chapter 4 - Informative Speaking

## *INFORMATION LITERACY: RESEARCHING & CITING SOURCES*

One of the most important skills you will learn in your *Public Speaking Fundamentals* Course is **information literacy,** defined as a set of skills helping you to "recognize when information is needed and have the ability to locate, evaluate, and use effectively the needed information" (American Library Association, 1989).

For public speaking, **information literacy** means you search for solid evidence to support your points when writing a speech and you effectively cite your sources when delivering your speech. You will always need to evaluate the **authorship, sponsorship and recency** of the documents you use. To help you begin to develop information literacy skills, **please answer** the following questions about the supporting material you will use in your next speech.

1. What are your main points that you will need to support?

2. What **types of supporting material** will you use to support each of your points? Will you need examples, statistics, or expert/lay testimony?

3. What sources will you use to obtain your supporting material?

    a. **Who published the information?** (sponsorship)
    - Does the source have a print outlet?
    - Is the source credible or is it biased? (e.g., Are you quoting a cigarette company which would be a biased source on cancer research?)

    b. **What is the publication date of each source?** (recency)
    - Does the date show that the source is current and timely?
    - Or is the source a foundational piece that sets a standard in the field? (e.g., Are you quoting a definition that has been established for decades?)

    c. **Who is the author of each source and what is the credibility and objectivity of the author?** (author & author's credibility)
    - Include the name and credentials of the author.
    - For author credentials or credibility, give the reason the author is an expert in the field or has first-hand experience with the topic and make sure the author is reasonably objective.

## References

American Library Association (1989). Presidential Committee on Information Literacy: Final Report. Retrieved May 6, 2020, from http://www.ala.org/ala/mgrps/divs/acrl/publications/whitepapers/presidential.cfm

Public Speaking Student Workbook

## CITING SOURCES ASSIGNMENT – INFORMATIVE SPEECH #2

**Objective:** To use information literacy skills to effectively find and cite sources.

**Instructions:** You will need to cite at least five sources in your second informative speech and use APA style for each citation in your list of reference (see Workbook p. 43-46). Follow these guidelines:

1. You can use **only one website source** that does not have a print outlet.

2. All of the sources that appear in your list of references must also appear in the **citation paragraphs in your preparation outline** and you must cite (say) each source when you deliver your speech.

3. The oral citation in your speech should contain the following **four elements**: 1) **Source** of the information, 2) **Author**, 3) **Author Credibility**, and 4) **Date** of article publication.

You will need to write a paragraph for each citation in your speech outline and include all four elements in each citation. **Be sure to highlight the citation paragraph in your outline**. Please complete the next page and attach this assignment to your preparation outline and your list of references. (Note: You would not say the bolded words in the parentheses when you deliver your speech.) See examples below.

### Examples of Citations for Public Speaking

**Internet Webpage Source with No Author (quotation)**
In fact, according to the *Federal Emergency Management Agency, FEMA* **(Source)**, on the website of the Department for Homeland Security **(Credibility)**, accessed on November 26, 2007 **(Date)**, "A tsunami is a series of huge waves that happen after an undersea disturbance, such as an earthquake or volcano eruption."

**Book (statistic)**
According to journalist **(Credibility)** Geoff Tibballs **(Author)**, who wrote *Tsunami: The Most Terrifying Disaster* book **(Source)**, in 2004 **(Date)** at least 300,000 people were swept to their deaths as the giant wave devastated everything in its path for over 2000 miles.

**Journal or Magazine Article (example)**
For example, in a *Canadian Geographic* article entitled *Wave Warning* **(Source)** written by geologist **(Credibility)**, Sarah Efron, **(Author)** published in October 2007**(Date)**: When a tsunami warning is sounded at least one half-hour in advance, most lives have been saved.

Chapter 4 - Informative Speaking

## CITING SOURCES FOR MY INFORMATIVE SPEECH #2

**Name**_____ **Speech Topic**_____

In the space provided below, please write a paragraph for each citation in your speech. Include all four elements (author, author's credibility, source, and date) in each citation (see the previous page for examples) and use a variety of types of sources. Then <u>attach this assignment to your preparation outline and references</u>. (Note: Make sure all citations appear in your preparation outline and all sources appear on your list of references.) **<u>You will use these citation paragraphs when you deliver your speech</u>**.

**Citation #1** (Book):




**Citation #2** (Journal or Magazine):




**Citation #3** (Brochure or Interview):




**Citation #4** (Newspaper or Media):




**Citation #5** (On-line):

Public Speaking Student Workbook

## *INSTRUCTOR EVALUATION FORM – INFORMATIVE SPEECH #2*

_____ TOTAL PERCENTAGE (%) POINTS     GRADE _____
NAME:_____ DATE: _____
TOPIC:_____ TIME: _____
KEY   EXCELLENT (5 ++)   GOOD (4 +)   FAIR (3 ✓)   WEAK (1 or 2 ✓--)   OMITTED (O)

### SPEECH OUTLINE & PREPARATION - 20 (%) POINTS
__Preparation Outline formatted (__sections labeled, __indented, __full sentences, __transitions, __references)
__Preparation Outline completed (__detailed points, __highlighted citation paragraphs, __references)
__Speaking Outline completed (__large cards, __dark print, __brief notes, __legible, large print)
__Audience Analysis attached (__questionnaire, __tally, __analysis summary)

### INTRODUCTION - 15 (%) POINTS
__Gained interest of audience (__captured attention for topic, __motivated audience to listen)
__Established your credibility (__why & __how you know about topic)
__Previewed main points in strategic order (__clear central idea) & fully introduced topic

### BODY = ORGANIZATION, DEVELOPMENT, & TRANSITIONS - 30 (%) POINTS
__Each main point easily identified, developed with details, and organized appropriately
__Sufficient and appropriate support used (____examples, ____testimony, ____statistics)
__Variety of sources cited (___book, ___magazine/journal, ___website, ___brochure, ___newspaper, __interview)
__Used complete citation paragraphs (__source, __credibility, __author, __date)
__Smooth connectives between main points (__used signal words, __used transitions)
__Related to and included audience (__referred to audience analysis, __adapted topic to audience)
__Optional: Use of slides or visual aids (__text minimal, __simple theme, __powerful images, __large fonts, __looked at display NOT the screen, __slide templates attached to outline)

### PRESENTATION & DELIVERY - 20 (%) POINTS
__Strong eye contact (__looked at all areas of the room, __looked only occasionally at notes or visual aid, __outline skillfully used, __eye contact was sustained throughout speech, __preparation & practice were evident)
__Effective use of voice (__sounded conversational, __used vocal variety, __used correct pronunciation/articulation, __used appropriate vocal rate – not too fast or too slow, __projected voice so all could hear, __paused effectively, few uhms)
__Expressive & used appropriate, audience-inclusive language (__sounded sincere, enthusiastic or passionate, __used language free of slang and profanity, __used language creatively, __imagery, __rhythm)
__Effective facial expression, gestures, & animation (__used appropriate movement – not stiff or pacing, __avoided distractions – little or no swaying, no gum chewing, __used professional posture, __used natural hand gestures)

### CONCLUSION & TIMING - 15 (%) POINTS
__Signaled ending (__used a signal word) & summarized main points (__restated each main point)
__Used vivid, interesting ending (__used quote or anecdote to make conclusion memorable)
__Adherence to time limit (__filled time requirement – not too short or too long)
_____ **Time of Speech**     _____ **Outline Handed in on Time**     _____ **Remained Informative**

### COMMENTS:

Chapter 4 - Informative Speaking

## *MY AUDIENCE ANALYSIS TALLY SUMMARY*

Summarize your audience's interest in, knowledge of, and attitude toward your topic in the space below. Explain how you will use this information to relate the topic directly to your audience. Then attach this page and your survey with tally to your outline.

1. From my tally, I learned that my audience members include the following:
   Knowledgeable about the topic         _____
   Not Knowledgeable about the topic     _____

2. My audience members have the following questions or concerns about my topic:

3. From my audience members, I learned the following and this is how I will adapt my speech to my audience (include how you will **change** or **plan your speech to** adapt to your audience's knowledge or concerns based on the survey):

   **Fixed-Alternative Questions**
   1) Summary of answers and how you will adapt your speech to your audience:


   2) Summary of answers and how you will adapt your speech to your audience:



   **Scale Questions**
   3) Summary of answers and how you will adapt your speech to your audience:


   4) Summary of answers and how you will adapt your speech to your audience:



   **Open-Ended Questions**
   5) Summary of answers and how you will adapt your speech to your audience:


   6) Summary of answers and how you will adapt your speech to your audience:


4. Write out a citation paragraph for a statistic, testimony, or example (see p. 67) from your survey that you will use in your speech (e.g., you might say, ""According to *my audience analysis survey, given to our class on October 12, 2018, I found…*").

Public Speaking Student Workbook

## *SELF-EVALUATION FORM FOR INFORMATIVE SPEECH #2*

NAME: _____ CLASS TIME: _____
TOPIC: _____ DATE: _____

**OBJECTIVES**:
1. To critically evaluate your own presentation.
2. To set goals to work on for your next speech in order to improve your presentation.

**INSTRUCTIONS**:
   View your recording one or more times. Use this evaluation form to analyze and evaluate the strengths and areas for improvement in your presentation.

1. **INTRODUCTION** (Gained Attention, Motivated Audience to Listen, Established Credibility, Previewed Main Points, Introduced Topic):

   Strengths:



   Areas for Improvement:



2. **BODY** (Manageable Number of Main Points, Main Points & Subpoints Developed with Sufficient Details, Effective Organizational Pattern, Smooth Transitions, Points Easily Identified, Easy to Follow):

   Strengths:



   Areas for Improvement:



3. **CONTENT AND USE OF SUPPORTING MATERIAL** (Sufficient and Appropriate Pieces of Supporting Material, Required Sources Cited--Examples, Quotations, & Statistics):

   Strengths:



   Areas for Improvement:

## Chapter 4 - Informative Speaking

4. **USE OF SLIDES & VISUAL AIDS** (Slides Used Minimal Text, a Simple Theme, Powerful Images, Large Fonts; You Looked at Display NOT the Screen AND All Visual Aids Were an Integral Part of Speech, Neat, Impactful, Clearly Visible by All & Used Effectively):

Strengths:


Areas for Improvement:



**5. DELIVERY & EXPRESSION** (Eye Contact, Conversational Delivery, Vocal Variety, Pauses (few uhms), Volume, Rate, Gestures, Enthusiasm, Vivid & Appropriate Language):

Strengths:


Areas for Improvement:


4. **CONCLUSION** (Signaled Ending, Summarized Main Points, Restated Importance of Topic to Audience, Used Vivid & Memorable Ending):

Strengths:


Areas for Improvement:


## OVERALL EVALUATION

5. Were you Audience-Centered and Sincere? Explain.

6. Were you satisfied or happy with your speech overall? Explain.

7. What would you do differently if you could give your speech again?

8. Describe ONE OR TWO goals you will work on to improve your next speech.

Public Speaking Student Workbook

## *USING VIVID LANGUAGE ASSIGNMENT*

NAME:_____ CLASS TIME:_____

**OBJECTIVES**:
1. To define descriptive language and stylistic devices that can add animation, imagery, and cadence (or rhythm) to your speeches.

2. To identify the many effective language devices used in variety of speeches.

**INSTRUCTIONS**:
In the space, define the following language techniques. Then, next to "Examples," please write down ways you can apply these techniques to your own speech.

**1. CONCRETE WORDS vs. CONNOTATIVE WORDS:**

   Examples:


**2. SIMILE:**

   Examples:


**3. METAPHOR:**

   Examples:


**4. REPETITION:**

   Examples:


**5. PARALLELISM:**

   Examples:


**9. ALLITERATION:**

   Examples:


**10. ANTITHESIS:**

   Examples:

Chapter 4 - Informative Speaking

## *FORMAL PREPARATION OUTLINE PEER REVIEW ACTIVITY*
NAME_____ Class Time_____
Review Partners Name_____
Partner's Speech Topic_____

**DIRECTIONS:**
Exchange a copy of your formal preparation outlines with your peer review partner. The goal of this activity is to give (and receive) critical, useful feedback which focuses on specific areas of your speech and speech outline. It is NOT helpful to say that the speech is "great" and needs no improvement. Consider the material we've covered to date and find ways for the speaker to incorporate elements of informative speaking for the items mentioned below.

### Read the introduction:
1. Did the speaker's introduction capture your attention and interest?
2. Does the introduction clearly establish the speaker's credibility to speak on the topic?
3. Does the introduction clearly preview <u>all</u> of the speaker's main points?

### Read the Body:
**Development:**
1. Can you identify the main points and transitions between points?
2. Is there appropriate number of main points (2-5)?
3. Is each main point supported and explained by the sub-points and supporting materials (statistics, examples, & testimony) with ample information?
4. Is there a similar word patterns for main points?
5. Is there a balance in the amount of time devoted to each main point?
6. Are the supporting materials cited appropriately?
7. Does the speaker relate to the audience using the audience analysis questionnaire?

**Organization:**
1. Are the main points organized using one of the organizational patterns appropriate for informative speaking?
2. Are each of the main points clearly distinct from the others?
3. Does the outline seem to flow in some logical way? (Tell the writer where you became confused about the sequence of the speech and mark the spot "unclear.")

### Read the Conclusion:
1. Is the conclusion clearly signaled with a sign-post?
2. Is there a summary of all main points and a restatement of the importance of the topic?
3. Is there a memorable ending (e.g., quotation, dramatic statement/story, etc.)?

### Preparation Outline & Overall:
1. Is the Specific Purpose & Central Idea clearly stated?
2. Are the main- & sub-points written in complete sentences?
3. Are the transitions clear & labeled?
4. Has the speaker incorporated enough supporting material?
5. Does the speaker correctly cite the supporting materials?
6. Has the speaker used proper grammar and punctuation?
7. Has the speaker incorporated the audience analysis survey?

Public Speaking Student Workbook

# 5

**Persuasive Speaking**

Assignments

Persuasive Mini-Speeches

Persuasive Speech Assignments

Topic & Research Reports

Evaluations

# Chapter 5 - Persuasive Speaking

## BASIC PERSUASION THEORY & CONCEPTS

**Definition of Persuasion:**
Persuasion is the process of changing, shaping, or reinforcing attitudes, beliefs, values, or behavior.

**Three Approaches to Persuasion:**
1. **Coactive Approach** — Bridges psychological distance between speaker and audience; relies on solid reasoning and strong evidence. The speaker builds rapport, identifies verbally and nonverbally with the audience, stresses benefits and consequences while encouraging the audience. (This is the approach we use in class; it is the most effective approach.)

2. **Combative Approach** — Creates a psychological distance between speaker and audience; relies on name-calling, derogatory remarks, threats, insults, put-downs, guilt-trips, or force. (We do NOT use this approach in class; it is the least effective approach for long- term results.)

3. **Expressivistic Approach** — Sees all persuasion as manipulative and exploitative and NOT worthy to be studied. (This approach is naive, self-deceptive, and irresponsible.)

**Persuasive Question:**
In order for there to be an issue for persuasion there must be a question that can be answered more than one way (i.e. there must be at least two sides to an issue).

**Three Types of Persuasive Speeches** (based on three types of persuasive questions):

1. **Questions of Fact** — Persuasive questions that deal with issues where the facts are inconclusive or where the future is predicted based upon present trends. The speaker advocates one side of the facts and draws a conclusion from the known facts.

2. **Questions of Value** — Persuasive questions that demand value judgments based upon a person's beliefs about what is right or wrong, better or best, good or bad, moral or immoral, fair or unfair. The speaker advocates a position by presenting standards for the value judgment and then applying those standards to the position of the speech.

3. **Questions of Policy** — Persuasive questions that deal with whether something should or should NOT be done. The speaker can seek passive agreement on a need for change (or no change) or can seek to motivate the audience to take a specific and often immediate action.

**Four Methods of Persuasion** (listeners are persuaded by speakers who use these methods):
1. Building Credibility
2. Using Evidence
3. Using solid Reasoning
4. Appealing to Emotions

**Definition of Argument:**
Argument is the reason(s) for believing something. You will need to use evidence as proof to support the reason(s). Effective persuasive speeches make strong arguments.

## Organizational Patterns for Persuasive Speeches
1. **Problem-Solution** (for Questions of Policy Speeches)
2. **Problem-Cause-Solution** (for Questions of Policy Speeches)
3. **Topical** (Good Reasons or Factual Categories for Questions of Fact or Value Speeches)
4. **Comparative Advantages** (for Questions of Policy Speeches when the audience already agrees that a problem exists and needs to be shown one solution is better than others)
5. **Monroe's Motivated Sequence** (for Questions of Policy Speeches that call for action)
6. **Refutation** (for Questions of Fact or Value or Policy Speeches when the speaker's position is under attack and the audience's objections to the proposals are known.)

## Need Fulfillment and Motivational Appeals
1. **Need Fulfillment** — We are motivated to respond to a persuasive message because it fills some need in our life. (See Maslow's Hierarchy of Needs.)

2. **Positive Motivational Appeal** — We are likely to respond to a persuasive message when the <u>benefits</u> of a proposal improve our quality of life and outweigh the costs.

3. **Negative Motivational Appeal** — We are likely to respond to a persuasive message if:
   1) We fear the results of not responding will threaten the safety of a loved one;
   2) We believe that danger or harmful results are real and close at hand; and
   3) The credibility of the speaker presenting the possible negative consequences is high.

## Basic Needs that Motivate People (based on Maslow's Hierarchy of Needs)
1. **Physiological Needs** — need for air, food, water, rest
2. **Safety Needs** — need for security, protection, and safety
3. **Social Needs** — need to belong, feel valued (respected), feel loved and cared for
4. **Self-Esteem Needs** — need for importance, esteem and recognition from others
5. **Self-Actualization Needs** — desire to achieve highest potential, ultimate satisfaction

**Other Needs include** (based on Eckerman updates):
- **Cognitive Needs** — need to know, discover, explore and learn
- **Aesthetic Needs** — need for beauty, order, cleanliness and a love of nature
- **Consistency Needs** — need for consistency in feeling, acting, and knowing (need to minimize internal inconsistencies in relationships, cognitions, beliefs, etc.)

## Principles of Persuasion
1. **Cognitive Dissonance** — When a persuasive message invites us to change, we will strive for balance in our thoughts in order to relieve any discomfort by 1) Attacking source credibility, 2) Focusing on only certain parts of the message we want to hear, 3) Seeking new information, 4) Ceasing to listen or 5) Changing.

2. **Consistency Principle** — We are more likely to be persuaded if the basic message or call for change is consistent with our attitudes, beliefs, values, and/or behaviors.

3. **Gradual Change Approach** — We are more likely to change our attitudes, beliefs, values, or behavior when change is called for gradually (not asking too much too soon).

# Chapter 5 - Persuasive Speaking

## *COACTIVE STRATEGIES FOR ADAPTING TO YOUR AUDIENCE*

### PERSUADING THE RECEPTIVE AUDIENCE
1. Establish a rapport and common ground with your audience early in your speech. Emphasize similarities. (i.e., common interests and background) with your audience.
2. Clearly state your speaking goal or purpose.
3. Use emotional examples and motivational appeals.
4. Call for an action (i.e., ask for a show of support from your audience).

### PERSUADING THE NEUTRAL AUDIENCE
1. Capture your audience's interest and attention in the introduction.
2. Establish rapport and common beliefs with your audience. Emphasize similarities/concerns.
3. Appeal to the needs of your audience's loved ones (the apathetic or unconcerned often become more concerned when a situation/problem affects a loved one).
4. Set modest goals; don't expect an immediate change in attitude or behavior.

### PERSUADING THE UNRECEPTIVE OR HOSTILE AUDIENCE
1. Be subtle; don't immediately announce your plan to change your audience's minds.
2. Establish a rapport and common ground with your audience early in your speech.
3. Work toward agreement on underlying concerns before you propose specific changes.
4. Establish your credibility and cite experts the audience will respect and accept.
5. Acknowledge opposing viewpoints to show that you respect and understand their position but then propose evidence and reasoning that demonstrates your position is better.
6. Set modest goals; don't expect major shifts in attitude or behavior.

### REFUTATION ORGANIZATIONAL PATTERN**
Use this organizational pattern when your position is under attack and you know your audience's objections to your solution. **Pick out two to four points to refute. For each point: (1) State the point you will refute; (2) Explain why the point is important to the audience; (3) Explain how you will refute it and then use credible sources;( 4) State your conclusion; and (5) Show how it discredits the position of the opposition. Then move to the next point you will refute.**

### EXAMPLE
I. Medicare reform is an important concern that we all need to be addressing today.
   A. Some would have you believe that Medicare reform will hurt our senior citizens; this is NOT true.
   B. I, like you, think that it is very important to protect our senior citizens who at one time were the working backbone of this country.
   C. Some statistical evidence shows that Medicare reform will actually protect our senior citizens.
      1. The National Department of Human Services shows that by 2025 the hospital trust fund will run out of money--it will hurt our elderly, but reforms will protect them.
      2. The US Secretary of Human Services recently said in (cite) that the latest Medicare reforms can save 22.5 billion dollars. Medicare reforms will help; No reforms will hurt.
   D. Therefore, the argument that Medicare reforms will hurt our seniors is NOT true.
   E. Without Medicare reforms there will be NO Medicare to help take care of our grandparents or parents and eventually you and me! Opposing Medicare reforms discounts the future.

*Coactive adaptation strategies adapted from: Simons, H. & Jones, J. (2012). *Persuasion in Society*.

## MINI SPEECH EXERCISE

**OBJECTIVES:**
1. To practice using the motivated sequence before you deliver your first formal persuasive speech.

2. To work with other students in the class and thus continue to promote a supportive class atmosphere.

**INSTRUCTIONS:**
Form a mini-speech team of 3 to 4 students. Your instructor will give you product picture. Study it carefully. Using the motivated sequence, write a mini-speech outline that attempts to sell this product to the audience. Use one to two sentences per sequence step. Divide up the speech so that each member presents some part of the speech. You can "make-up" examples, testimony, and statistics to support your ideas, but be sure to use realistic positive and negative motivational appeals or fear appeals. Work quickly and efficiently because the mini-speeches will be presented today. (Use the outline below.)

**PRODUCT/SERVICE:**

**SPECIFIC PURPOSE:** To persuade my audience to buy _____.

**CENTRAL IDEA:** You should buy/use (product/service) because_____.

**INTRODUCTION:** ATTENTION STEP (get listener's attention): (Also state your credibility and preview your points.)

**BODY:**
  I. NEED STEP or Problem (Establish need for product — do not mention product.):

  II. SATISFACTION STEP or Solution (Identify how your product will satisfy their need.):

  III. VISUALIZATION STEP or Benefits and Consequences of NOT purchasing (Give the audience a sense of what will happen if they do or do NOT buy your product):

  A. BENEFITS: Positive Motivational Appeals — Show audience how wonderful it would be if they
     buy.

  B. CONSEQUENCES: Negative Motivational or Fear Appeals--Remind the audience how awful
     or hard it will be for them if they do NOT buy or use your product.

**CONCLUSION:** CALL TO ACTION STEP: (Offer the audience clear steps they should take on how and where to buy this product. Also, signal your ending and summarize your main points.)

Chapter 5 - Persuasive Speaking

## *MOTIVATED SEQUENCE MINI-SPEECH INSTRUCTOR FEEDBACK FORM*

SPEAKERS:_____ DATE: _____
TOPIC: _____ TIME: _____

_____ (%) POINTS EARNED

### CHECKLIST

### INTRODUCTION
___ ATTENTION STEP: Captured audience's attention __ Related topic to audience's needs
___ Established group credibility __ Prepared audience for rest of speech (preview)

### BODY: ORGANIZATION & DEVELOPMENT
___ NEED STEP: Clearly explained problem and related it audience's need
___ SATISFACTION STEP: Clearly explained solution and satisfaction of need
___ VISUALIZATION STEP: Presented strong benefits and/ or consequences
___ Used strong motivational appeals
___ Clearly used motivated sequence organization __ Used smooth transitions
___ Used sufficient & cited supporting material (__examples, __statistics, __quotations)

### CONCLUSION
___ Signaled the end with a signpost __ Summarized main points __ Motivated audience
___ ACTION STEP: Boldly called audience to take a specific action __ Needed a stronger call
___ Used a memorable ending or dramatic appeal __ Needed a more memorable ending

### DELIVERY, LANGUAGE, & IMPRESSION
___ Eye contact for all was (circle): Excellent  Very Good  Good  Average  Fair  Poor
___ Needed to look at all areas of the room ___ Read too much of speech
___ Sounded conversational __ Sounded passionate and persuasive
___ Projected voice so all could hear ___ Spoke too softly ___ Spoke too loudly
___ Used audience-inclusive language __ Avoided slang or profanity

### OVERALL REQUIREMENTS
___ Fulfilled time requirement __ Each student contributed equal time & effort
___ Outline was complete __ Points were labeled with speakers' names

### OVERALL RATING OF SPEECH & USE OF MONROE'S MOTIVATED SEQUENCE
**(circle):**  Excellent        Good        Average        Fair        Poor


### OVERALL COMMENTS

Public Speaking Student Workbook

*TOPICS FOR PERSUASIVE SPEECHES WORKSHEET*

NAME_____ CLASS TIME _____

**OBJECTIVE**: To generate topics for persuasive speeches.

**INSTRUCTIONS**:
Since at least one of your persuasive speeches will involve showing your audience there is a problem (or need for change) and then suggesting a solution, you will need to generate topics for a problem-solution organizational pattern. To generate topics, read articles or editorials and listen to news stories for local, regional, or national problems. Suggested resources include: 1) News Reports or Editorial sections in the university, city, regional or other newspaper; 2) Recent issues of magazines such as *Time, Newsweek, Consumer Reports*; 3) News programs on radio or television.

**REQUIREMENTS AND EVALUATION CRITERIA**:
1. Jot down five (5) problems, which could serve as speech topics, in the space below.
2. Write your solution to each problem, based upon what you read and will propose.
3. Write a specific action you could ask others to take in order to begin to achieve your proposed solution.

   1. Problem:
      Solution:
      Action:

   2. Problem:
      Solution:
      Action:

   3. Problem:
      Solution:
      Action:

   4. Problem:
      Solution:
      Action:

   5. Problem
      Solution:
      Action:

Chapter 5 – Persuasive Speaking

## *FACT, VALUE, POLICY ASSIGNMENT*

Name _____

Read the five specific purpose statements (SPs) for persuasive speeches below and for each one, determine if the speech would likely concern a question of fact, a question of value, or a question of policy. Then rewrite the SP so that it is appropriate for a speech about one of the other two kinds of questions. For instance, if the original purpose statement represents a question of FACT, write a new specific purpose statement on the same topic that represents either a question of policy or a question of value.

1. **To persuade my audience to donate to the Red Cross.**
   *Does this specific purpose deal with a question of fact, value, or policy?*
   *Rewritten specific purpose statement:*

2. **To persuade my audience that pornography is a major cause of violence against women.**
   *Does this specific purpose deal with a question of fact, value, or policy?*
   *Rewritten specific purpose statement:*

3. **To persuade my audience that the State of Nebraska should put greater emphasis on solar power to meet the state's energy needs.**
   *Does this specific purpose deal with a question of fact, value, or policy?*
   *Rewritten specific purpose statement:*

4. **To persuade my audience that drinking bottled water is a waste of time, money and effort.**
   *Does this specific purpose deal with a question of fact, value, or policy?*
   *Rewritten specific purpose statement:*

5. **To persuade my audience that working for Lyft is better than working for Uber.**
   *Does this specific purpose deal with a question of fact, value, or policy?*
   *Rewritten specific purpose statement:*

Public Speaking Student Workbook

## *MONROE'S MOTIVATED SEQUENCE SPEAKER CHECKLIST*
### *Persuasive Dyad Speech #1*

Please use this checklist to prepare your dyad speech. It will help you get the best grades. When you turn in your outline, please include this completed checklist with it.

## Speech

- The speech topic relates to an event, product, or service available in our city or state.
- The speech follows the motivated sequence of events.
  - Attention: In the introduction, stimulate your audience's interest in the topic.
  - Need/Problem: In the first main point, show a serious problem with an existing situation (using strong evidence) and tie it to your audience's needs.
  - Satisfaction/Solution: In the second main point, clearly present a solution to the problem (plan of action) and explain how it meets your audience's needs and is workable.
  - Visualization: In the third main point, present positive and negative images of what could happen if your plan is and/or is NOT adopted.
  - Call for Action: In the conclusion, appeal to your audience to take action, be specific and give them something to do immediately.
  - The event, product, or service is not mentioned until the satisfaction/solution step.
- Maslow's Hierarchy of Needs has been incorporated into the speech.

## Outline and Supporting Material

- The outline follows the ten rules for outlining found of workbook page 42 (label, use complete sentences, highlight supporting material, etc.).
- Each main point of the outline is labeled with the person's name that will be responsible for delivering that part of the speech.
- The outline contains <u>six pieces</u> of supporting material.
  - At least one statistic is cited.
  - At least one testimony/opinion is cited.
  - At least one example is cited.
- At least three different types of sources are cited.
- All six citation paragraphs are complete with source, author, credibility, and date.
- Wikipedia is NOT used as a source.
- References are in APA format and are attached to the outline.
- Slides followed the guidelines, Workbook p. 54 & templates submitted with outline.

## Practice/Preparation

- The speech has been practiced with all members present.
- The speech met the time limit guidelines.
- Each speaker has his/her own set of speaking cards.

# Chapter 5 – Persuasive Speaking

## *EXAMPLE OF DYAD PERSUASIVE SPEECH OUTLINE*

**Name:** Terry Howe and Michelle Rio  **Title:** Use the Metro Area Transit
**Organizational Pattern:** Monroe's Motivated Sequence
**General Purpose:** To persuade (to take action)
**Specific Purpose:** To persuade my audience to use the Metro Area Transit (MAT) for three reasons.
**Central Idea:** You should use the Metro Area Transit for three reasons: 1) MAT is an economical way to travel, 2) MAT is reliable and safe, and 3) MAT saves on the use of gas and foreign oil.

**Introduction: (Terry)**
**Attention:** The Frozen Over Story: 6 AM winter car breakdown causes frustrations in getting to class/work.
**Importance:** Owning a car is expensive & environmentally harmful, but there is an alternative.
**Credibility:** We both use alternative transportation to school since 1867 when our choice first began running according to authors Lawrence & Cottrell in their 1997 book, The Gate City: A History of Omaha).
**Preview:** Today, we will cover an auto alternative that is economical, reliable, & saves on the use of oil.
**Body**
I. **(Need/Problem)** College students need money for housing, food & transportation. (Terry)
   A. Cars are expensive to own and operate.
      1. Maintenance, insurance, licensing and gas can cost thousands of dollars per year.
      2. UNO students have to pay for expensive and inconvenient on-campus parking.
         a. UNO Parking Rules & Regulations Brochure reports student parking costs $125 per year.
         b. The brochure says UNO sells more permits than spaces; no guarantee for a spot you want.
   B. Cars can fail you, just when you need them.
      1. AAA.com, in 5-7-2009. reports helping about 3.2 million stranded motorists in the summer.
      2. Examples: Cars that don't start cause you to lose money, grades, jobs, social elevation.
   C. Driving a car helps consume much of our environmental resources.
      1. "$CO_2$ emissions from U.S. cars & trucks totaled 314 million metric tons in 2012." It's like releasing burning coal in train 50,000 miles. Klebnikov in Environmental Defense Newsletter, Dec. 2016.
      2. The EPA Fact Sheet in 2012 reported $CO_2$ emissions from cars is 20.4 lbs. per gallon.
(**Transition:** To avoid the costs, problems, and impact of driving, we have a solution for you.)
II. (**Satisfaction/Solution**) The public transportation system, (MAT) is inexpensive, reliable, & efficient.
   A. MAT is cheap and helps you save money. (Michelle)
      1. For $1.25, you can ride 15 miles on a bus compared to 10 miles in a car MAT website, 6-1-10)
      2. Factoring in the cost of car maintenance, insurance, and a car payment for even a Toyota Prius, you would save $9,062 per year (American Public Transportation Association report, 10-6-13).
   B. MAT is reliable.
      1. MAT has a fleet of 110 buses according to Glen Bradley, Maintenance Supervisor, 11-3-14.
      2. If a MAT bus breaks down, another bus will be there within 45 minutes Bradley says.

(**Transition**: Public transportation clearly offers benefits so next you can visualize other outcomes.)

III. (**Visualization/Practicality**) Public transportation offers benefits without negative consequences.
   A. Riding a bus benefits, you with productive, less stressful commute time. (Michelle)
      1. Picture yourself finishing a paper or studying for a test without having to focus on driving. OR
      2. You could be annoyed by the traffic, looking for a parking spot; you can't enjoy the view.
   B. Using public transportation helps our environment and our country become less oil dependent.
      1. Picture how good you feel by knowing that you are creating 95% less carbon dioxide per mile.
      2. By riding a bus you can be confident that you are saving twice the fuel (2010, Time, Layton)
**Conclusion:** (Terry)
**Signpost/Summary:** In conclusion, using MAT saved money, reduces stress, & increases productivity.
**(Call to Action):** Starting tomorrow, walk to the bus stop, pay the $1.25, and ride the bus to campus.
**Memorable Ending:** Take time to enjoy the ride and the money saved to enjoy your favorite night spot.
**References:** l Larsen, L., & Cottrell, B. (1997). History of Omaha. Nebraska Press: Omaha, NE
*Ideas adapted from original student dyad outline by Travis King & Mike Rizza (used by permission).

## MOTIVATED SEQUENCE GROUP OUTLINE WORKSHEET

**Group Members**:
**Topic**:
**Specific purpose**: to persuade my audience to _____.
**Central idea**: after listening to my speech, the audience members should ____.

**Introduction**: *(name of student responsible for this*
**Attention step** (get listener's attention):
**Motivator** (relate to audience. How will your product/service benefit them?):
**Credibility**:
**Preview**:

**Body**: *(name of student responsible for this section_____)*
**I. Problem or need step** (establish a clear need for the product, but do not mention the product):
    A.
        1. (include supporting material)
        2.
    B.
        1. (include supporting material)
        2.
**Transition**:

**II. Solution or satisfaction step** ((identify how your plan will satisfy the need): *(name_____)*
    A.
        1. (include supporting material)
        2.
    B.
        1. (include supporting material)
        2.
**Transition**:

**III. Visualization step** or benefits and consequences of not purchasing (give the audience a sense of what will happen if they do or do not buy your product): *(name of student _____)*
    A. **Benefits**: positive motivational appeals--remind audience how wonderful it will be if they buy.
        1.
        2.
    B. **Consequences**: negative motivational appeals--remind audience how awful it will be for them if they do not buy.
        1.
        2.

**Conclusion**: *(name of student responsible for this part*
**Signal ending with a signpost**:
**Summarize main points**:
**Call to action step**: give clear steps on how to and where to buy product.
**References**:

# Chapter 5 – Persuasive Speaking

## POSIBLE TOPICS FOR PERSUASIVE SPEECHES

This is a list of speech topics that students have used effectively in previous classes. Use this list as a way to brainstorm your own unique ideas for topics.

- Attend TEDxUNO
- Donate to the Food Pantry
- Online privacy
- Support local businesses
- Internet regulation
- Use MavRide
- Ride the city bus
- Take the Whole30 Challenge for Health
- Become a Vegan
- Eat a Keto or Paleo diet
- Stop cyber bullying
- Learn a second language
- Begin investing early in life
- Renewable energy
- Midwifery vs. hospital delivery
- Kindles vs. iBooks
- Workplaces should offer exercise programs
- You should plan and use a budget
- Music education is beneficial
- Use the rock climbing wall
- Our city needs a light rail system
- Art is a way to relieve stress and anxiety
- People in the US should watch more foreign films
- Diet pills are a dangerous to your health
- Visit a museum
- Stop Sex-trafficking
- Tanning beds are dangerous
- The display of the Ten Commandments
- Community vegetable gardens
- Mixed-Fit Dance
- Cosmetic surgery
- Pilates vs. other forms of exercise
- Dating Apps
- The Media's portrayal of beauty
- Increase mental health spending
- Buy at farmer's markets
- Use Pinterest
- Diet soda causes weight gain
- Buy a hybrid car
- Require high school speech classes
- Become an exchange student
- You should adopt a child
- Trades should be offered in high school
- Genetically modified food
- Fitbit vs. Apple Watch
- Flu shots
- Vaccinations
- Travel/study abroad
- Eat organic meats
- Women and the draft
- NCAA basketball vs. NBA basketball
- Limit your use of social media
- Try CrossFit
- Exercise daily
- Learn a second language
- Music heals
- Honking should be punished
- Limit your use of antibiotics
- You should adopt a pet
- Alternative medicine
- Take vitamins
- Aspartame hurts your brain
- Student debt forgiveness
- Organ donation
- Switch from cable to Netflix
- Paternity leave
- Ban certain dog breeds
- Sustainable farming
- Cardio vs. strength training
- Go to Junk-stock
- Universities should cut out Gen Eds
- Student athletes should be paid
- Homeschooling
- Destination weddings
- Uber vs. Lyft
- Online piracy
- Eat breakfast daily
- Meditate daily to reduce stress
- Enroll in a graduate certificate program

Public Speaking Student Workbook

## *PERSUASIVE DYAD SPEECH #1: THE MOTIVATED SEQUENCE*
## *Inspiration to Do, Buy, Attend or Support a LOCAL Non-Profit*

**SPEECH DUE DATE:**
**OUTLINE DUE DATE:**
**TIME LIMIT**: 3 to 4 minutes per person (6 to 8 minutes total)
**OBJECTIVES**
To practice using persuasive theory and persuasive strategies, especially Monroe's Motivated Sequence and strong motivational appeals (benefits and consequences for the audience).
1. To continue developing public speaking skills learned in informative speaking.
2. To work with other students and thus continue to promote a supportive class atmosphere.

**INSTRUCTIONS**

This is a dyad (partner) speech so you will need to form a speech team with another person. Together choose an event, product, or service available in our city or state to promote or a non-profit to support. Your goal is to urge your audience to attend an event or use a service (e.g., tickets to the Community Playhouse, the Children's Museum, an art exhibit, a concert or music performance, the zoo, a hockey season pass, a local health club/spa membership, an outdoor adventure center activity, an Internet service, a cooking course series, a sorority/fraternity membership, etc.) or support a non-profit organization (e.g., volunteer for Hands on Network-Omaha, contribute to an Omaha homeless shelter, donate to the Food Bank, etc.). You and your partner will create a 6 to 8-minute speech following the motivated sequence and using strong positive and negative motivational appeals, based on Maslow's Hierarchy of Needs. On the outline, please label each of the five steps and make sure you use at least SIX PIECES of recent evidence (examples, testimony, and statistics) to support your ideas. Presentational slides are optional but if used, must follow the guidelines on Workbook p. 54. Divide up the speech so that each member presents some part of the speech. Each student will be expected to speak for 3 to 4 minutes. Speaking dates will be assigned and all speaking date rules apply. See outline example, p. 84 and outline planning worksheet, p. 85.

**EXPECTATIONS & EVALUATION CRITERIA**
1. **Select a partner and choose a local topic.** Dyads in the same class are not allowed to use the same topic as another dyad chooses.
2. **Prepare and write your speech outline following Monroe's Motivated Sequence.**
   a. **Fully develop each step** to show your knowledge of the Motivated Sequence.
   b. **Clearly label each STEP** (*Attention, Need/Problem, Satisfaction/ Solution, Visualization, Call for Action*) and **clearly label each part with the speaker's name.**
3. **Use motivational appeals based on Maslow's Hierarchy of Needs** or Basic Needs.
4. **Use six pieces of supporting material**, including **three (3) different local** sources types (e.g., brochures, newspapers, articles) and all three types (e.g., examples, quotations, statistics).
5. **Each Dyad will turn in one SP/CI (p. 93) and one preliminary preparation outline** (p. 85).
6. **Before your speech, each Dyad will turn** in the following:
   a. **One completed preparation outline** (follow format on p. 91-92),
   b. **One list of references, and One Citing Sources Assignment (p. 94).**
7. **Each speaker may use two note cards** (5" x 8") for writing down key words to jog the memory while delivering the speech. Practice your speech with your cards so you know it well.
8. **Each dyad will deliver the speech together—together you will come to the front of the room** on the day of the class presentations. One at a time, you will step forward and present your part.
9. **Each person/speaker will individually complete and submit a self-evaluation.**
10. The speech is worth 100 points. The writing and preparation of the speech will be scored as a dyad-team while delivery will be scored individually. Evaluation criteria include: Introduction, Use of the Motivated Sequence, Organization, Transitions, Content Development, Supporting Material, Use of Language, Conclusion, Delivery, Time Limits, Audience-centeredness, and Outlines.

Chapter 5 – Persuasive Speaking

## *DYAD CONTRACT FOR PERSUASIVE SPEECH #1*

Working in dyads requires your commitment to do your part. To assist you in this process, you will need to read the following contract and sign it as your agreement to be part of the dyad. If you break your commitment, you may receive little, if any points, for the speech.

I agree to the following:
1. I will build respect for my partner in this speech.
2. I will communicate with my partner.
3. I will keep in contact with my partner via email or phone.
4. I will work out a schedule when we can meet.
5. I will commit to show up for class to work on the speech.
6. If I do not come to class or work with my partner, I understand I may forfeit some or all of the points for this speech.
7. Together we will write and combine our efforts in one outline for our speech and then submit the one outline to our instructor.
8. Together, we will have a minimum of six sources for the speech.


_____        _____
*Signature*                                                          *Date*

Public Speaking Student Workbook

## *PERSUASIVE SPEECH #1 (INDIVIDUAL): THE MOTIVATED SEQUENCE*

**SPEECH DUE DATE**:
**OUTLINE DUE DATE**:
**TIME LIMIT**: 4 to 6 Minutes

**OBJECTIVES**:
1. To convince your audience to take a specific, immediate action on a solution to a problem.
2. To use the five steps of Monroe's Motivated Sequence as your organizational pattern.
3. To use effective motivational appeals (positive and negative), a variety of supporting material, descriptive language, and effective delivery techniques.

**INSTRUCTIONS**:
Your first formal persuasive speech is designed to help you develop and practice persuasive speaking skills using Monroe's Motivated Sequence. All steps in the motivated sequence must be covered in your formal preparation outline, and you should use positive and negative motivational appeals, especially in the Visualization Step. You may choose a local issue. A variety of topics would be appropriate. For example, you might try to persuade your audience to become organ donors, to buy Levi Jeans, to become a Big Sister/ Big Brother, to support a local museum, to volunteer at a homeless shelter, or to become a student regent). Presentational slides are optional but if used, please follow the *Presentational Slides Assignment & Guidelines* on Workbook page 54, submit your slide show with your outline and email your slide show to your instructor before your speech.

**REQUIREMENTS AND EVALUATION CRITERIA**:
1. Your speech should be effectively organized, outlined, introduced, and concluded.

2. Your speech should be supported with at least 5 pieces of supporting materials. Examples, statistics, and quotations need to be cited in 1) Your Speech, 2) Your Speech Outline, and 3) Your References. You must use a minimum of three (3) different TYPES of sources in your list of References. Remember to incorporate your source citations into your speech delivery (e.g. "Time magazine reported in March 2017, that...").

3. Your speech should include these five steps of Monroe's Motivated Sequence:
   1) ATTENTION. In the introduction, stimulate your audience's interest in the topic.
   2) NEED/PROBLEM. In the first main point, show a serious problem with an existing situation (using strong evidence) and tie it to your audience's needs.\
   3) SATISFACTION/SOLUTION. In the second main point, clearly present a solution to the problem (plan of action) and explain how it meets your audience's needs and is workable.
   4) VISUALIZATION. In the third main point, present positive and negative images of what could happen if your plan is or is NOT adopted. Tell your audience what will benefit them directly if they adopt your plan; tell your audience what negative consequences could happen (affecting them or their family members) if they do NOT adopt your plan.
   5) CALL FOR ACTION. In the conclusion, appeal to your audience to take action--be specific and give them something to do immediately.

# Chapter 5 – Persuasive Speaking

4. Your speech must be audience-centered. Try to relate to your audience in each step.

5. Your preparation outline (including the References) must be prepared and TYPED following formal outline format. Your preparation outline is due one class period before all speeches are scheduled. Your speaking note cards are due immediately following your presentation.

6. Your speech must be delivered extemporaneously from notes. Do NOT prepare a speech manuscript; do NOT memorize a manuscript. Please use only a few note cards (5" x 8") for your speaking notes. Practice your speech several times before the day of your presentation.

7. This assignment is worth a possible 100 points. Evaluation criteria include: Introduction, Use of the Motivated Sequence Organizational Pattern, Use of Transitions, Content Development, Use of Supporting Material, Use of Vivid Language, Conclusion, Delivery, Overall--Time Limit, Audience-centeredness, and Outlines.

**LIST OF ITEMS DUE FOR PERSUASIVE SPEECH #2**
_ Completed Persuasive Speech Checklist (p.83)
_ Typed Preparation Outline–with highlighted citation paragraphs
_ Typed References
_ Completed Library Assignment for Persuasive Topics (p. 80)
_ Completed Citing Sources Assignment for Persuasive Speech #1 (p. 94)
_ Slide Templates attached, if slides are used (See Workbook p. 54 for guidelines and p. 226 for
   Templates)
_ Speaking Card(s)

**Bring your workbook to class for these two forms**
_ Instructor's evaluation form
_ Peer feedback forms
_ Mail slideshow to you instructor so it will be ready to use.

Public Speaking Student Workbook

## *MONROE'S MOTIVATED SEQUENCE & PROBLEM SOLUTION FORMAT*

**TOPIC**:
**SPECIFIC PURPOSE**: To persuade my audience to _____ (take this action to solve this problem).
**CENTRAL IDEA**: My audience should _____ (take this action) because the problem is _____, the solution is _____, and the benefits/consequences are _____.

**INTRODUCTION**:
**ATTENTION STEP** (include a powerful attention-getter):
**Motivator** (Relate to audience. Give audience a reason to listen – what they can gain):
**Credibility**:
**Preview**: Preview your proposition in a way that does not give away your solution.

**BODY**:
**I. NEED or PROBLEM** (Establish a clear need or problem in MAIN POINT ONE):
   A. Describe the Need or Problem.
      1. Describe the effects of the problem (include signs and symptoms).
         a. statistics or quotations (with citations)
         b. examples that relate to audience (with citations)
      2. Explain the probable cause(s) and/or relevant history of the problem.
         a. statistics or quotations (with citations)
         b. examples that relate to audience (with citations)
**Transition**:
**II. SATISFACTION or SOLUTION** (Describe the solution in MAIN POINT TWO):
   A. Describe your plan in detail.
      1. Describe how your solution will be implemented.
      2. Explain what actions need to be taken now (and later) to solve the problem.
      3. Describe the cost, time, and efforts needed for the solution
   B. Explain how your solution addresses the problem.
      1. Explain how your solution addresses the problem.
      2. Show evidence to support your plan.
         a. statistics or quotations (with citations)
         b. examples that relate to audience (with citations)
**Transition**:
**III. VISUALIZATION or PRACTICALILTY** (Describe benefits and consequences for your audience in MAIN POINT THREE):
   A. DESCRIBE BENEFITS: (Use Positive Motivational Appeals relates to your audience)
      1. Use imagery to help the audience picture the results result if they follow the plan.
      2. Use an example to describe how a similar plan has worked. Cite sources.
   B. DESCRIBE CONSEQUENCES: USE Negative Motivational and Fear Appeals.
      1. Use imagery to help audience envision how bad it could get if the problem continues.
      2. Use examples of negative impact. Cite sources.

**CONCLUSION**:
   **Signal ending** with a signpost and **Summarize Main Points:**
   **CALL TO ACTION STEP** (if MMS is used): Give the audience clear steps to take now.
   **Leave the Audience with a memorable ending**
   **References**:

# Chapter 5 – Persuasive Speaking

## *INSTRUCTOR EVALUATION FORM – INDIVIDUAL PERSUASIVE SPEECH #1*

_____TOTAL PERCENTAGE (%) POINTS  _____GRADE
NAME:_____ DATE: _____
TOPIC:_____ TIME: _____

KEY   EXCELLENT (5 ++)   GOOD (4 +)   FAIR (3 ✓)   WEAK (1 or 2 ✓--)   OMITTED (O)

### SPEECH OUTLINE & PREPARATION - 15 (%) POINTS
__Preparation Outline Format (__sections labeled, __indented, __full sentences, __transitions, __references)
__Preparation Outline Details (__detailed points, __highlighted citation paragraphs, __references)
__Speaking Outline Format & Details (__large cards, __dark print, __brief notes, __legible, print)

### INTRODUCTION - 15 (%) POINTS
__Attention Step (__captured attention for topic, __motivated audience to listen)
__Established Speaker Credibility (__why & __how you know about topic)
__Prepared Audience for Body of Speech (__clear central idea or __preview of main points)

### BODY = ORGANIZATION, DEVELOPMENT, & TRANSITIONS - 35 (%) POINTS
__Need Step (__clearly explained problem, __developed ideas, __related to audience's needs)
__Satisfaction Step (__clearly explained solution, __practicality shown)
__Visualization Step (__presented strong benefits, __strong consequences, __imagery)
__Sufficient and appropriate support used (____examples, ____testimony, ____statistics)
__Various sources cited (____book, ____magazine/journal, ____website, ____brochure, __newspaper, ____interview)
__Smooth connectives between main points (__used signal words, __used transitions)
__Related to and included audience (__adapted topic to audience, __questionnaire, __tally and paragraph)
__Optional: Use of slides/visual aids (__text minimal, __simple theme, __powerful images, __large fonts, __looked at display NOT the screen, __slide templates attached to outline)

### PRESENTATION & DELIVERY - 20 (%) POINTS
__Strong eye contact (__looked at all areas of the room, __looked only occasionally at notes, __outline skillfully used, __eye contact was sustained throughout speech, __preparation & practice were evident)
__Effective use of voice (__sounded conversational, __used vocal variety, __used correct pronunciation/articulation, __used appropriate vocal rate – not too fast or too slow, __projected voice so all could hear, __paused effectively, few uhms)
__Expressive & used appropriate, audience-inclusive language (__sounded sincere, enthusiastic or passionate, __used language free of slang and profanity, __used language creatively, __imagery, __rhythm)
__Effective facial expression, gestures, & animation (__used appropriate movement – not stiff or pacing, __avoided distractions – little or no swaying, no gum chewing, __used professional posture, ___used natural hand gestures)

### CONCLUSION & TIMING - 15 (%) POINTS
__Signaled ending (__used a signal word) & summarized main points (__restated each main point)
__Action Step (__called for audience to take specific, immediate action, __used a memorable ending)
__Adherence to time limit (__filled time requirement – not too short or too long)
_____**Time of Speech**  _____**Outline Handed in on Time**

### COMMENTS:

Public Speaking Student Workbook

# TOPIC, SPECIFIC PURPOSE, CENTRAL IDEA & RESEARCH REPORT
# PERSUASIVE SPEECH #1 – MONROE'S MOTIVATED SEQUENCE

Name: _____ Class Time: _____

**Goal for this Speech** (based upon the last speech--e.g. increase eye contact, increase gesturing, slow down, add more citations):

**Topic**:

**Rationale** (Why did you choose this topic?):

**General Purpose**: TO PERSUADE (using Monroe's Motivated Sequence)

**Specific Purpose**:

**Central Idea**:

**Organizational Pattern:** Monroe's Motivated Sequence

**Ideas for Main Points** (include at least three points written in complete sentences):

I. NEED STEP (PROBLEM):


II. SATISFACTION STEP (SOLUTION):


III. VISUALIZATION STEP (PRACTICALITY with benefits & negative consequences):


**Ideas for the Introduction or Conclusion**:

    ATTENTION STEP:

    SLIDES:

    CALL TO ACTION STEP:

Commitment: I have read the dyad contact on p. 88 and agree to do my part.
I understand that if I do not fulfill the contract, I will lose some or all of the points for this speech.

Signed: _____

Chapter 5 – Persuasive Speaking

## CITING SOURCES ASSIGNMENT – PERSUASIVE SPEECH #1

Name_____ Speech Topic_____

**Objective:** To use information literacy skills to effectively find and cite sources.

**Instructions:** You will need to cite at least five sources in your second persuasive speech and in your outline. Please use a variety of sources (books, brochures, magazines, newspapers, on-line, interviews) and APA style (see Workbook p. 46). You need to follow these guidelines:

1. You can use **only one Internet webpage source** that does not have a print outlet.
2. All of the sources that appear in **your list of references** must also appear in **parenthesis in your preparation outline** and you must cite each source **orally**.
3. The oral citation in your speech should contain the following elements: 1) **Source** of the information, 2) **Author**, 3) **Author Credibility**, and 4) **Date** of article publication.

In the space below, please write a paragraph for each of the six citations you will use in your persuasive speech. Include all four elements in each citation and attach this assignment to your outline and references. See Workbook p. 66-67 for additional information and examples.

### Example: Book (Testimony--Quotation)
According to college professor and textbook author **(Credibility)** Stephen Lucas **(Author)**, who wrote *The Art of Public Speaking Handbook* **(Source)** in 2018 **(Date)**, "understanding the principles of persuasion" are "vital to being an informed citizen and consumer."

**Citation #1:**

**Citation #2:**

**Citation #3:**

**Citation #4:**

**Citation #5:**

**Citation #6:**

Public Speaking Student Workbook

## *INSTRUCTOR EVALUATION FORM – DYAD PERSUASIVE SPEECH #1*

NAMES:_____ DATE:_____
TOPIC:_____ TIME:_____

KEY   EXCELLENT (5 ++)   GOOD (4 +)   FAIR (3 ✓)   WEAK (1 or 2 ✓--)   OMITTED (O)

**Group Points**

### SPEECH OUTLINE & PREPARATION - 10 (%) POINTS
__Preparation Outline formatted (__sections labeled, __indented, __full sentences, __transitions, __references)
__Preparation Outline completed (__detailed points, __highlighted citation paragraphs, __references)

### INTRODUCTION - 15 (%) POINTS
__Attention Step (__captured attention for topic, __motivated audience to listen)
__Established your credibility (__why & __how you know about topic)
__Prepared audience for body of speech (__clear central idea or __preview of main points)

### BODY = ORGANIZATION, DEVELOPMENT, & TRANSITIONS - 30 (%) POINTS
__Need Step (__clearly explained problem, __developed ideas, __related to audience's needs)
__Satisfaction Step (__clearly explained solution, __practicality shown)
__Visualization Step (__presented strong benefits, __strong consequences, __imagery)
__Sufficient and appropriate support used (___examples, ___testimony, ___statistics)
__Variety of sources cited (___book, ___magazine/journal, ___website, ___brochure, ___newspaper, __interview/expert)
__Smooth connectives between main points (__used signal words, __used transitions)
   __Optional: Use of visual aids (__visible, __neat, __interesting, __effective timing, __passed only at end)

### CONCLUSION & TIMING - 10 (%) POINTS
__Signaled ending (__used a signal word) & summarized main points (__restated each main point)
__Action Step (__called for audience to take specific, immediate action, __used a memorable ending)
   _____Outline Handed in on Time   _____ Persuasive   _____Time of Speech

GROUP POINTS_____ 65 (%) TOTAL POINTS

---

**Individual Delivery Points**

NAME:_____ DELIVERY, TIMING, & ADAPTATION = 35(%) POINTS
__Strong eye contact __Effective use of voice (and passion) __Appropriate, creative language
__Gestures/animation __Fulfilled time limit __Speaking card (brief, legible) __Adapted to audience
DELIVERY POINTS _____ + GROUP POINTS _____ = TOTAL SPEECH POINTS _____

NAME:_____ DELIVERY, TIMING, & ADAPTATION = 35(%) POINTS
__Strong eye contact __Effective use of voice (and passion) __Appropriate, creative language
__Gestures/animation __Fulfilled time limit __Speaking card (brief, legible) __Adapted to audience
DELIVERY POINTS _____ + GROUP POINTS _____ = TOTAL SPEECH POINTS _____

NAME:_____ DELIVERY, TIMING, & ADAPTATION = 35(%) POINTS
__Strong eye contact __Effective use of voice (and passion) __Appropriate, creative language
__Gestures/animation __Fulfilled time limit __Speaking card (brief, legible) __Adapted to audience
DELIVERY POINTS _____ + GROUP POINTS _____ = TOTAL SPEECH POINTS _____

# Chapter 5 – Persuasive Speaking

# Public Speaking Student Workbook
## *SELF-EVALUATION FORM for PERSUASIVE SPEECH #1*

NAME:_____ CLASS TIME: _____

TOPIC: _____ DATE: _____

**OBJECTIVES**
1. To critically evaluate your own presentation.
2. To set goals to work on for your next speech in order to improve your presentation.

**INSTRUCTIONS**

View your recording one or more times. Use this evaluation form to analyze and evaluate the strengths and areas for improvement in your presentation. For the dyad speech, evaluate the entire speech based on use of the motivated sequence. For the delivery category, please evaluate only your own delivery (not your partner's delivery).

1. **INTRODUCTION** (STRONG ATTENTION STEP—Gained Attention & Motivated Audience to Listen, Established Credibility, Previewed Main Points, Introduced Topic):

    Strengths:

    Areas for Improvement:

2. **BODY** (Effective and Clear Use of the Motivated Sequence Pattern, STRONG NEED STEP Clearly Explained & Related to Audience, CLEAR SATISFACTION STEP with Practicality, STRONG VISUALIZATION STEP with Motivational Appeals, Smooth Transitions):

    Strengths:

    Areas for Improvement:

3. **CONTENT AND USE OF SUPPORTING MATERIAL** (Used Sufficient and Appropriate Pieces of Supporting Material from a Variety of Sources--at Least Three Different Types & Not Dependent on Internet Webpage Sources, Required Sources Cited--Examples, Quotations, & Statistics):

    Strengths:

    Areas for Improvement:

4. **DELIVERY & EXPRESSION** (Strong Eye Contact, Conversational Delivery, Vocal Variety, Pauses (few uhms), Volume, Rate, Gestures, Enthusiasm, Vivid & Appropriate Language):
    Strengths:

    Areas for Improvement:

## Chapter 5 – Persuasive Speaking

5. **USE OF SLIDES & VISUAL AIDS** (Slides Used Minimal Text, a Simple Theme, Powerful Images, Large Fonts; You Looked at Display NOT the Screen AND All Visual Aids Were an Integral Part of Speech, Neat, Interesting, Clearly Visible by All & Used Effectively):
Strengths:

Areas for Improvement:

6. **CONCLUSION** (Signaled Ending, Summarized Main Points, STRONG CALL TO ACTION STEP, Restated Importance of Topic to Audience, Used Vivid & Memorable Ending):
Strengths:

Areas for Improvement:

## OVERALL EVALUATION

7. Were you Audience-Centered and Sincere? Explain.

8. Were you satisfied or happy with your speech overall? Explain.

9. What would you do differently if you could give your speech again?

10. Describe ONE OR TWO goals you will work on to improve your next speech.

## DYAD EVALUATION (Please evaluate your dyad partner. This will be confidential.)

11. How did you split up the speech project?

12. Rate your partner (1=rarely/never, 2=occasionally/ sometimes, 3=all/most of the time)
    Did fair share of work,
    Contributed to planning/ideas
    Was cooperative and finished agreed tasks
    Was available for communication
    Was positive and helpful
    Contributed to overall speech success

13. Rate your contribution as compared to your partner or group members.
    Choose one: ___Excellent ___Very Good ___ Good ___ Average ___ Poor

14. Explain your reasoning for your self-evaluation score:

Public Speaking Student Workbook
*PERSUASIVE SPEECH ASSIGNMENT #2*
*A PROPOSITION OF FACT, VALUE OR POLICY*

**SPEECH DUE DATE:**
**OUTLINE DUE DATE:**
**TIME LIMIT:** 5 to 7 Minutes

## OBJECTIVES
1. To persuade a professional audience on a proposition of fact, value, or policy; thus, convincing your audience to change their attitudes, values, beliefs, or behaviors.
2. To use effective methods of persuasion: building credibility; using evidence; using logical reasoning; and appealing to emotions.
3. To use effective delivery techniques, descriptive language techniques, audience analysis, and a variety of supporting material.
4. To effectively use presentational software and slides to enhance your presentation.

## INSTRUCTIONS
Your second formal persuasive speech is designed to help you further develop persuasive speech making skills, especially designed for a professional audience. Your goal is to present a persuasive speech that convinces a professional audience to agree with your proposition. The central idea of your speech will be a proposition of fact, value, or policy. For a fact proposition, you will assert a particular view of the facts based on standard knowledge and research—you might assert that something is true or false or that something did happen or is likely to happen based on evidence or patterns. (Your evidence is presented in the main points and often organized topically.) For a value proposition, you will assert an opinion that something is "better" or "best" based on clear standards and evidence. (Your main points are often divided into standards and justification of your opinion based on the standards.) For a policy proposition, you will assert that something should or should not be done with clear problem, solution, and practicality points. (You would likely organize your main points using a problem-cause-solution or a motivated sequence pattern.) A variety of topics would be appropriate. For example, you might try to persuade us that learning a new language at any age has benefits, that music heals, that exercise is essential for mental prowess, that energy drinks are really medicine, that it is better to eat fruit than drink juice, that is it best to drink purified water than consume sodas or coffee, that swimming is the best type of exercise, that fairytales should be rewritten for the next generation, that you should use a time-table to manage your life, that you should practice relaxation to improve your health, that you should follow a Keto diet to lose weight, that you should stop sunbathing.

## REQUIREMENTS AND EVALUATION CRITERIA
1. Your speech must address a question of fact, value, or policy. Please write at the top of your outline which type of question you will address. Remember when speaking about a proposition of fact, you must give special attention to reasoning and presenting your side of the facts. When speaking on a proposition of value, you must identify your standards and justify your judgment in light of those standards. When speaking about a proposition of policy, you must show a clear problem, solution with practicality/workability, and benefits for your audience.

2. Your speech should be effectively organized, outlined, introduced, and concluded. Include a slide show of six to eight slides following the Guidelines on Workbook p. 54. Then submit the

## Chapter 5 – Persuasive Speaking

slide templates with your outline and email your instructor your slideshow so it will be available for the day you speak.

3. Your speech should be supported with at least <u>five (5) pieces</u> of supporting materials. Your examples, statistics, and quotations need to be cited in 1) Your Speech, 2) Your Speech Outline, and 3) Your References. You must use a minimum of <u>three (3) different types</u> of sources in your References (only one Internet webpage source). Remember to incorporate the citations into your speech delivery using your citation paragraphs.

4. Your speech should include vivid language. Please use and label (underline) all stylistic devices, including metaphors, similes, alliteration, parallelism, antithesis, or repetition.

5. You must be audience-centered. You should adapt your speech to your audience based upon the results of your audience analysis survey. You will administer an audience analysis questionnaire with at least two fixed-alternative questions, two scale questions, and two open-ended questions in class before giving your speech. Attach a copy of your typed <u>questionnaire with a tally</u> of your survey and a <u>summary for each question (see p. 104)</u> describing what you learned and how you will adapt to your audience.

6. Your preparation outline with the References must be TYPED in formal outline format and submitted **one class period** before all speeches are scheduled or you cannot speak. Your speaking note cards are due immediately following your presentation.

7. Your speech must be delivered extemporaneously from notes. Do NOT prepare a speech manuscript; do NOT memorize a manuscript. Please use no more than three (3) note cards (5" x 8") for your speaking notes. Practice your speech several times before your presentation.

8. Your slide show and visual aid must be an integral part of your speech. Use ONLY six to eight slides and do NOT read from the screen. Please email your slide show to your instructor before you speak. Follow the presentational slides guidelines on Workbook p. 54.

9. After class, view your recorded speech and do a self-evaluation of your presentation. Your self-evaluation is due the class period after the last round of persuasive speeches.

10. This assignment is worth a possible 200 points. Evaluation criteria include: Clear Persuasive Proposition, Introduction, Motivational Appeals, Credibility Appeals, Supporting Materials, Transitions, Presentational Slides, Content Development, Organization, Conclusion, Delivery, Audience-centeredness with Reference to Audience Analysis and Outlines.

**LIST OF ITEMS DUE FOR PERSUASIVE SPEECH #2**
　_ Completed Persuasive Speech #2 Checklist (p. 105)
　_ Typed Preparation Outline –with highlighted citation paragraphs & _ References
　_ Audience Analysis Questionnaire with Tally
　_ Audience Analysis Summary – describing how you will adapt your speech to
　　your audience (p. 104)
　_ Completed Citing Sources Assignment (p. 102)
　_ Slide Templates attached to Outline, and slideshow emailed to instructor in advance
　　of your speech

**Bring your workbook to class for these two forms:**
　_ Instructor's evaluation form _ Peer feedback form

Public Speaking Student Workbook
## *PERSUASIVE SPEECH #2 — A PROPOSITION OF FACT, VALUE, OR POLICY*

Name_____ Class Time_____

**MY PERSONAL GOAL FOR THIS SPEECH** (based upon my self-evaluation of my last speech--e.g., increase eye contact, increase gesturing, slow down):

**Topic**:

**Rationale** (Why did you choose this topic?):

**TYPE OF PERSUASIVE QUESTION** (Circle one: FACT, VALUE, OR POLICY):

**STATE THE PERSUASIVE QUESTION YOU ARE ADDRESSING** (e.g., Should you drink diet soda?):

**Specific Purpose**:

**Central Idea**:

**Organizational Pattern**:

**Ideas for the Introduction**:

**Ideas for Main Points*** :
*__Policy__ speeches consider using Problem/Solution, Problem/Cause/Solution, or Monroe's Motivated Sequence.
*__Value__ speeches use standards and justification for the main points or as part of each main point.
*__Fact__ speeches use topical organization to give reasons with evidence as to why your proposition is true.
I.


II.


III.


**Ideas for the Conclusion**:


**Emotional Appeals**:

**Ideas for the Slides (required)**:

Chapter 5 – Persuasive Speaking

## CITING SOURCES ASSIGNMENT—PERSUASIVE SPEECH #2

Name_____ Speech Topic_____

**Objective:** To use information literacy skills to effectively find and cite sources.

**Instructions:** You will need to cite at least five sources in your second persuasive speech and in your outline. Please use a variety of types of sources and APA style (see Workbook p. 46). You need to follow these guidelines:

1. You can use **only one** webpage/**internet source** that does not have a print outlet.
2. All of the sources that appear in **your list of references** must also appear in **parenthesis in your preparation outline** and you must cite each source **orally**.
3. The oral citation in your speech should contain the following elements: 1) **Source** of the information, 2) **Author**, 3) **Author Credibility**, and 4) **Date** of article publication.

In the space below, please write a paragraph for each of the five citations you will use in your persuasive speech. Include all four elements in each citation and attach this assignment to your outline and References. See Workbook p. 66-67 for additional information and examples.

### Example: Book (Testimony--Quotation)
According to college professors and textbook authors **(Credibility)** Steven A. Beebe and Susan J. Beebe **(Authors),** who wrote *A Concise Public Speaking Handbook* **(Source)** in 2014 **(Date),** "To advocate a particular view or position successfully, you must understand your listener's attitudes, beliefs, values, and behavior."

**Citation #1** (Book):


**Citation #2** (Journal or Magazine):


**Citation #3** (Brochure or Interview):


**Citation #4** (Newspaper or Media):


**Citation #5** (On-line):

Public Speaking Student Workbook

## *INSTRUCTOR EVALUATION FORM – PERSUASIVE SPEECH #2*

_____TOTAL PERCENTAGE (%) POINTS    _____GRADE

NAME:_____ DATE: _____
TOPIC:_____ TIME: _____
TYPE OF PERSUASIVE SPEECH _____ORGANIZATIONAL PATTERN _____
KEY: EXCELLENT (5 ++)   GOOD (4 +)   FAIR (3 √)   WEAK (1 or 2 √--)   OMITTED (O)

### SPEECH OUTLINE & PREPARATION - 15 (%) POINTS
__Preparation Outline Format & Details(__sections labeled, __indented, __full sentences,
  __transitions, __detailed points, __highlighted citation paragraphs, __reference list,
  __ clear organizational pattern, __slide templates attached to outline)
__Speaking Outline Format & Details (__large cards, __dark print, __brief notes, __legible print)
__Audience Analysis Questionnaire, Tally & Summary (__questionnaire, __tally, __ summary)

### INTRODUCTION - 15 (%) POINTS
__Gained interest of audience (__captured attention for topic, __motivated audience to listen)
__Established speaker credibility (__why & __how you know about topic)
__Prepared audience for body of speech (__clear central idea or __preview of main points)

### BODY = ORGANIZATION, DEVELOPMENT, & TRANSITIONS - 35 (%) POINTS
__Effective Organization & Development (__points easily identified, __points developed with
  Details __appropriate organization with MMS [__need, __satisfaction, __visualization] OR
  PS [__problem, __solution with __cause or __practicality] OR CE [__cause, __effect] OR
  VALUE [__standards, __met standards] OR FACT [__clear grouping of fact categories])
__Sufficient support used to make logical argument (___examples, ___testimony, __statistics)
__Used complete citation paragraphs (___source, ___credibility, ___author, ___date)
__Variety of sources cited (__book, ___magazine, ___website, ___brochure, ___newspaper)
__Used connectives between main points (__used signal words, __used clear transitions)
__Related to/ included audience (__adapted to audience, __referred to audience analysis,
  __ remained coactive)
__Effective use of presentational slides (__text minimal, __simple theme, __powerful images, __large
  fonts, __looked at display NOT the screen, __visible, __impactful __effective timing)

### PRESENTATION & DELIVERY - 20 (%) POINTS
__Strong eye contact (__looked at all areas of the room, __looked occasionally at notes, __outline
  skillfully used, __eye contact sustained throughout speech, __preparation & practice evident)
__Effective use of voice (__sounded conversational, __used vocal variety, __used correct
  pronunciation/articulation, __used appropriate vocal rate – not too fast or too slow, __projected
  voice so all could hear, __paused effectively, few uhms)
__Expressive & used appropriate, audience-inclusive language (__sounded sincere, enthusiastic or
  passionate, __ free of slang and profanity, __ language with __emotion, __imagery/rhythm)
__Effective facial expression, gestures, & animation (__used appropriate movement – not stiff or
  pacing, __avoided distractions – little or no swaying, no gum chewing, __used professional
  posture, __used natural hand gestures)

### CONCLUSION & TIMING - 15 (%) POINTS
__Signaled ending (__used a signal word) & summarized main points (__restated each main point)
__Used vivid, interesting ending (__used quote or anecdote to make ending memorable)
__Adherence to time limit (__filled time requirement – not too short or too long, __remained
persuasive)

_____ Time of Speech     _____Outline Handed in on Time

**COMMENTS:**

Chapter 5 – Persuasive Speaking

## *MY AUDIENCE ANALYSIS TALLY SUMMARY*

Summarize your audience's interest in, knowledge of, and attitude toward your topic in the space below. Explain how you will use this information to relate the topic directly to your audience. Then attach this page and your survey with tally to your outline.

1. From my tally, I learned that my audience members include the following:
   Receptive:   _____
   Neutral:     _____
   Hostile:     _____

2. My audience members have the following questions or concerns about my topic:

3. From my audience members, I learned the following and this is how I will adapt my speech to my audience (include how you will **change** or **plan your speech to** adapt to your audience's knowledge, concerns, or objections based on the survey):

   **Fixed-Alternative Questions**
   1. Summary of answers and how you will adapt your speech to your audience:

   2. Summary of answers and how you will adapt your speech to your audience:

   **Scale Questions**
   3. Summary of answers and how you will adapt your speech to your audience:

   4. Summary of answers and how you will adapt your speech to your audience:

   **Open-Ended Questions**
   5. Summary of answers and how you will adapt your speech to your audience:

   6. Summary of answers and how you will adapt your speech to your audience:

4. Write out a citation paragraph for a statistic, testimony, or example from your survey that you will use in your speech (e.g., you might say, ""*According to my audience analysis survey from November 16, I found...*").

Public Speaking Student Workbook

## *PERSUASIVE SPEECH #2 — SPEAKER CHECKLIST*

Please use this checklist to prepare your first speech. It will help you get the best grade possible. When you turn in your outline, please include this completed checklist with it.

### Preparation Outline

- Clear Specific Purpose and Central Idea that is persuasive
- Typed formal outline format using the ten rules for outlining — see Workbook p. 42
  - Labeled all parts of outline, used complete sentences, and used Roman numerals, letters, and numbers.
  - Highlighted <u>five citation paragraphs</u>
  - References in APA format - attached to the outline.
- Audience analysis questionnaire, tally with summary, p. 104, attached

### Introduction

- Attention: In the introduction, stimulate your audience's interest in the topic and explain how it will help them. (Please do not begin: "Today I am going to tell you ….")
- Credibility: State how you know about the topic and why you are interested in it.
- Preview: Express the main points of your speech.

### Speech Body Development and Supporting Material

- Used identifiable organizational pattern — motivated sequence, topical-facts, or standards
- Used at least five <u>pieces</u> of supporting material.
  - At least one statistic is cited.
  - At least one testimony/opinion is cited.
  - At least one example is cited.
- Three different types of sources are cited. Wikipedia is NOT a source.
- Effectively cited - five citation paragraphs- with source, author, credibility, and date.
- Used a quotation or statistic from your audience analysis.

### Conclusion

- Sign post: Signal ending (e.g., use words such as, *in review, in conclusion,* etc.)
- Summary: Summarize all main points in your speech.
- Importance to Audience: State how your information is helpful for your audience.
- Memorable Ending: Use a statistic, illustration, example, quotation, etc.
- Call to Action: Invite an action response.

### Note Cards, Slides & Speech Practice

- Note cards are completed — brief notes, large lettering, labeled, and numbered.
- I practiced the speech to verify it falls within the time limit of 4 to 6 minutes.
- I practiced using the note cards.
- I practiced using presentational slides that included minimal text, a simple theme, powerful images, large fonts, and I looked at the computer display NOT the projector screen.

# Chapter 5 – Persuasive Speaking

Public Speaking Student Workbook
*SELF-EVALUATION FORM FOR PERSUASIVE SPEECH #2*

NAME:_____ CLASS TIME: _____
TOPIC: _____ DATE: _____

**OBJECTIVES**
1. To critically evaluate your own presentation.
2. To set goals to work on for your next speech in order to improve your presentation.

**INSTRUCTIONS**:

View your recording one or more times. Use this evaluation form to analyze and evaluate the strengths and areas for improvement in your presentation.

1. **INTRODUCTION** (Gained Attention, Motivated Audience to Listen, Established Credibility, Previewed Main Points or Clearly Introduced Topic):

   Strengths:


   Areas for Improvement:


2. **BODY** (Manageable Number of Main Points & Sub-points, Effective Organizational Pattern, Smooth Transitions, Points Easily Identified, Easy to Follow):

   Strengths:


   Areas for Improvement:


3. **CONTENT AND USE OF SUPPORTING MATERIAL** (Each Main Point Developed with Appropriate Details & Justification, Solid Reasoning, Sufficient Pieces of Supporting Material, Required Sources Cited--Examples, Quotations, & Statistics, Variety of Sources Used—at least three different types):

   Strengths:


   Areas for Improvement:

## Chapter 5 – Persuasive Speaking

4. **USE OF MOTIVATIONAL OR EMOTIONAL APPEALS** (Use of Vivid & Emotional Language, Clear Benefits & Negative Consequences Related to Audience):
Strengths:

Areas for Improvement:

5. **DELIVERY & EXPRESSION** (Eye Contact, Vocal Variety, Pauses (few uhms), Volume, Rate, Gestures, Enthusiasm, Appropriate Language):
Strengths:

Areas for Improvement:

6. **USE OF SLIDES** (Slides Used Minimal Text, a Simple Theme, Powerful Images, Large Fonts, Used Effectively - Looked at Display NOT the Projector Screen; and the Visual Aids Were Impactful & Clearly Visible by All):
Strengths:

Areas for Improvement:

7. **CONCLUSION** (Signaled Ending, Summarized Main Points, Restated Importance of Topic to Audience, Used Vivid & Memorable Ending or Strong Final Appeal):

Strengths:

Areas for Improvement:

## OVERALL EVALUATION

8. Were you Audience-Centered and Sincere? Explain.

9. Were you satisfied and happy with your speech overall? Explain.

10. What would you do differently if you could give your speech again?

Public Speaking Student Workbook

# 6

# CEREMONIAL SPEAKING

COMMEMORATIVE SPEAKING SPEECH #5

GUIDELINES

COMMEMORATIVE SPEECH PLANNING WORKSHEET

ORGANIZATIONAL PLAN

EVALUATION FORMS

CRITICAL ANALYSIS

Chapter 6 – Ceremonial Speaking

## *COMMEMORATIVE SPEAKING, SPEECH #5*

**SPEECH DUE DATE:**
**OUTLINE DUE DATE:**
**TIME LIMIT:**

This speech is designed to help you develop ceremonial speaking skills. As you plan your speech, please follow the requirements, guidelines, and principles on the next few pages.

Ceremonial speeches are delivered at special ceremonies of life, such as:
- Weddings
- Funerals
- Graduations
- Retirement/anniversary/birthday celebrations
- Award presentations

General categories of ceremonial speeches include:
- Commemorative speeches – pay tribute to a person, group, institution, or event
- Speeches of introduction – create a welcoming, enthusiastic climate for a speaker
- Speeches of presentation – present someone with an award, gift, or public recognition
- Speeches of acceptance – show gratitude and humility when receiving an award

## GENERAL REQUIREMENTS

1. Your speech should be effectively organized, introduced, and concluded.

2. Your preparation outline must be prepared and TYPED following formal outline format. Your preparation outline is due one class before all speeches are scheduled. Your speaking note card is due immediately following your presentation.

3. Your speech must be delivered extemporaneously from brief notes. Do not prepare a speech manuscript. Please use only one (1) note card (5" x 8") for your speaking notes. Maintain a lot of eye contact with your audience. It should seem as though you know the subject well, and can talk about the person, event, or award without hesitation.

4. Practice your speech in front of a mirror or friends to increase eye contact, enthusiasm, sincerity, and conversational delivery. Demonstrate that you know the subject of your speech well by not relying heavily on your speaking note card.

5. After class, view your recorded speech and do a self-evaluation. Your self-evaluation is due the class period after the last round of ceremonial speeches.

6. This assignment is worth a possible ___ points. Evaluation criteria include: Introduction, Organization and Use of Transitions, Content Development (See specific speech type for guidelines. May include biographical or historical information, character qualities or values, principles to be learned, achievements, etc.), Conclusion, Extemporaneous and Conversational Delivery, Time Limit, Audience-centeredness, and Outlines.

## GENERAL GUIDELINES FOR CEREMONIAL SPEECHES

### Commemorative Speeches
Choose a person, group, institution or event to honor or celebrate in a commemorative speech. For example, you might honor a former teacher at a retirement ceremony, praise a person or group who has made a significant contribution to your life or the lives of others, eulogize a person who has died, celebrate the anniversary of your college, business, or church, or memorialize a significant event (e.g., the end of World War II). Your goal is to provide some biographical or historical information about the person, group, or event in a way that focuses on such things as character qualities, acts of service, or contributions to the community or others.

### Tips for Commemorative Speeches
1. Begin with an intriguing introduction or attention getter (e.g., use an example, metaphor, or quotation, etc.).
2. Mention the event or occasion for your speech. You should use the word "tribute" or "celebration" to give respect to the subject you are honoring.
3. Briefly mention your connection to your subject, without focusing on yourself.
4. Give the background of the person, institution, or event so the audience will know why your subject is praiseworthy. Include historical information, character qualities, acts of service, and/or contributions to the community.
5. Go beyond only historical details; try to inspire your audience with respect for the subject (e.g., mention obstacles overcome, purity of motives, superiority of accomplishments, etc.).
6. Include principles and/or values to be learned from the subject. For example, a eulogy would include life-long accomplishments of the person who has died and what values or principles we can learn from his/her life.
7. Include vivid examples or personal stories that show the character qualities, events, or acts you are honoring. Select examples that will not embarrass the person.
8. Be selective and choose the best examples and details to illustrate your points.
9. Use stylistic language devices such as simile, metaphor, parallelism, or alliteration (see textbook for ideas) to arouse interest, emotion, admiration, and/or consolation.
10. Conclude your speech appropriately. For a eulogy, express sorrow and sympathy. For other situations, express appreciation, admiration, or good wishes for the future.

### Speeches of Introduction
Choose a real person to introduce as a speaker. For example, you might choose an author, a political leader (local or national), a representative of a student organization, or a motivational speaker. Your goals are to provide some biographical information about the person and his or her accomplishments, to identify the topic of the person's speech, and to explain why the person's speech topic is important for the audience.

# Chapter 6 – Ceremonial Speaking

**Tips for Speeches of Introduction**
1. Ask the speaker, in advance, what she or he would like you to emphasize in the introduction.
2. Make sure you can pronounce the speaker's name correctly and have all the facts right.
3. Make every effort to help the speaker feel welcome.
4. Begin with an intriguing attention getter (e.g., use an example, metaphor, or quotation).
5. When appropriate, briefly mention the occasion for the presentation and your connection to the subject (without focusing on yourself).
6. Use points that include biographical information about the speaker, including several achievements or contributions.
7. Highlight the topic of the speech. Explain its importance to the audience.
8. Explain why the speaker is qualified to speak on the topic.
9. Use vivid language to highlight the speaker's qualifications.
10. To create drama and anticipation, avoid mentioning the speaker's name until the last moment.
11. Conclude your speech appropriately by welcoming the speaker. Use his or her name and the title of the speech. Invite applause.

## Speeches of Presentation

Choose a real person to honor with an existing award, gift, or recognition from a local, regional, or national organization/ institution. For example, you might present an award to a member of an organization, a scholarship recipient, or a winner of an athletic competition. Your goal is to mention accomplishments or contributions to show the audience why the recipient is worthy of the award.

**Tips for Speeches of Presentation**
1. Research your award and recipient thoroughly so you know what you are presenting and why you are presenting the award.
2. Begin with an intriguing introduction or attention getter (e.g., use an example, metaphor, or quotation, etc.).
3. Next explain the purpose for the award and why the award is being given. You may want to mention the occasion for the presentation.
4. Explain the history or significance of the award.
5. Mention your connection to the subject briefly, without focusing on yourself.
6. Introduce the recipient and tell the audience why he or she is receiving the award.
7. Use points that include several achievements or contributions the recipient has made. (You will speak glowingly of the recipient.)
8. Include interesting examples of the achievements related to the award.
9. Use vivid language that highlights the character qualities and outstanding acts of the recipient.
10. If the award was won in a competition, acknowledge the tough contest and praise the other competitors.
11. Conclude your speech appropriately by congratulating the recipient. Use his or her name and the name of the award. Invite applause from the audience.

## Speeches of Acceptance

Choose an existing award from a local, regional, or national organization/institution that you will accept. For example, you might choose to be awarded a certificate at your job, a particular scholarship or academic award, an athletic award, or any other award you would especially like to receive. Your goals are to express gratitude for the honor and values the award represents, to thank those who presented you with the award, to thank those who made it possible for you to receive the award, and to praise the runners-up or competitors.

### Tips for Speeches of Acceptance
1. Research the award/honor thoroughly so you know what you are receiving and why you are receiving it.
2. Accept the award with graciousness and humility. Be modest and grateful.
3. Introduce your speech by expressing your gratitude for the award.
4. Express your awareness of the award's deeper meaning by highlighting the values the award represents.
5. Express gratitude to those who presented you with the award.
6. Express gratitude to those who made it possible for you to receive the award. (If a teacher, parent, family member, coach or others made it possible for you to receive the award, thank them. Especially mention some who are present at the awards ceremony. Try not to mention so many people that you detract from your speech by taking too much time.)
7. Include vivid examples or personal stories to illustrate the meaning of the award or your experiences related to the award.
8. Choose language that fits the occasion. Slang and jokes are usually out of place because they suggest you do not value the award or take the occasion seriously.
9. If the award involved a competition, praise your competitors for making it hard to decide who would receive the award. However, do not apologize for receiving the award.
10. Conclude with a memorable statement or brief example about the award, organization, or event.

### Checklist of Items Due
___ Typed Preparation Outline

___ Speaking Note Card(s)

___ Bring your workbook with you for your **instructor's evaluation form**

Chapter 6 – Ceremonial Speaking

## *COMMEMORATIVE SPEECH PLANNING WORKSHEET*

1. What kind of speech are you planning?
   - ✓ Toast
   - ✓ Eulogy
   - ✓ Tribute (praise) to a person, group, or institution

2. Who or what will you praise? _____ (If you choose a person you do not personally know, you will do research to find out about the person's life.)

3. What key character qualities, attributes, virtues, or accomplishments will you praise (e.g., honesty, perseverance, kindness, faithfulness, love, or an accomplishment made this person worthy of recognition)? Select two or three:
   _____

4. Describe the audience for this speech. How have or could these virtues, attributes, or accomplishments relate to, inspire, encourage, or motivate this audience? How will you relate this speech to your audience?
   _____

5. Formulate a goal (specific purpose) for your speech. You may use this format:
   To praise _____ (person, institution) for qualities of _____
   _____ (or accomplishments) _____

6. Briefly describe 2 to 3 specific biographical examples (stories) that demonstrate these attributes, virtues, or accomplishments. Interesting details make a speech vivid and memorable, so describe a picture that will make an impact on your audience. Include at least one personal example that reflects how this person or institution impacted your life.

   a. **Virtue/Accomplishment Example #1:**

   b. **Virtue/Accomplishment Example #2:**

   c. **Virtue/Accomplishment Example #3:**

7. Look back at your specific purpose. Do your examples demonstrate the attributes or accomplishments you plan to praise? _____ If not, how will you adjust your *goal* or your *examples*?
   _____

8. Search quotations at the library website to find a quotation that relates to the virtues or accomplishments you are extolling. Write the quotation here: _____
   _____

9. Use the following guidelines to organize an effective commemorative speech and develop your main points. Remember to keep your comments brief and focused on your purpose. Always use creativity to make the speech unique, meaningful, and memorable.

# Public Speaking Student Workbook

## *ORGANIZATION FOR COMMEMORATIVE SPEECHES*

**INTRODUCTION** (Purpose, Quotation, Preview)
- State your purpose (to honor the life of a special person, to praise an accomplishment, to celebrate a wedding) and acknowledge audience ("What an occasion to celebrate—Tom and Sarah's wedding day! I am so glad you could be here to celebrate with them!").
- Use your quotation at the beginning or end of your speech. Quotations are a memorable way to open or close.
- Preview the virtues, attributes, or accomplishments ("There are so many things Grandpa taught me during his life, but two that stand out are his patience and caring").

**BODY** (Virtues, Attributes or Accomplishments for Main Points & Examples for Each)
- Develop each main point to praise a different virtue or accomplishment. Use your examples to demonstrate the honoree's attributes, etc. (e.g., Tom's sense of humor has helped many of his friends—myself included—to make it through stressful days during college. Once he painted my bar of soap with clear finger nail polish so that when I tried to use it, it wouldn't lather! Laughing over his antics was a great way to relieve stress, and I know that Tom's sense of humor will be a great asset to Tom and Sarah's married life!").
- Include examples of how you personally benefited from or were impacted by this person, but do not focus on what you have done. (Doing so will seem like you are inappropriately praising yourself when the focus should be on the honoree.)
- Deliver the examples in an interesting way. Cut out any unnecessary information
- Use an appropriate tone for the occasion.
  - Eulogy—express sorrow and grief; praise accomplishments of the person's life.
  - Toast—give best wishes, congratulations, hope for the future.
  - Tribute—show appreciation; inspire the audience through the example.

**CONCLUSION** (Signal Word, Virtue/Attribute Summary, Memorable Ending)
- Use a word to signal the ending and then review the key attributes being praised.
- Conclude with a meaningful sentiment for the occasion ("Let's raise our glasses to the bride and groom!" or "I will never forget Grandpa's influence on me, a 12-year-old boy for whom he always had time"). Consider using a stirring quotation that summarizes the attributes or accomplishments you are honoring.

**DELIVERY**
- Your delivery should include a great deal of eye contact and a highly conversational, sincere tone (as a speaker, you are praising a person you personally know well, and you should deliver it in a way that reflects that).
- Vivid language (parallelism, repetition, antithesis, alliterations, concrete words, metaphors, similes) should be used to highlight important points and to make the speech memorable.
- After you have planned your ceremonial speech, practice delivering it several times.
- Be sincere in your delivery, and genuinely express your praise, honor, and respect.

Due date for Worksheet(s): _____ This speech is worth a possible _____ points.

# Chapter 6 – Ceremonial Speaking

Public Speaking Student Workbook

## *TOPIC, SPECIFIC PURPOSE AND CENTRAL IDEA REPORT*
## COMMEMORATIVE SPEECH

Name:_____Class Time:_____

Topic: _____

**Rationale** (Why did you choose this topic?):

**General Purpose**: TO HONOR/ PAY TRIBUTE

**Person, Event, or Institution for Your Tribute:**

**Specific Purpose:**

**Central Idea:**

**Introduction:**

**Main Points** (Refer to Guidelines on Workbook p. 113):

I.



II.



III.



**Conclusion:**

# Chapter 6 – Ceremonial Speaking

Public Speaking Student Workbook
*COMMEMORATIVE MINI-SPEECH EVALUATION FORM*

**Student Name** _____ **Date**_____ **Time**_____

KEY: Excellent (5 ++)  Good (4 +)  Fair (3 ✓)  Weak (1 or 2 ✓--)  Excluded (0)

Type of Commemorative or Ceremonial Speech (circle one):
- Toast
- Eulogy
- Tribute to a person or group of people or
- Tribute to an institution or idea

___ Introduction
    ___ Stated Purpose
    ___ Explained Personal Connection to Topic
    ___ Used Attention-getting Quotation or Example
    ___ Previewed Virtues, Attributes, or Accomplishments

___ Main Points & Supporting Material
    ___ Main Points were Attributes, Virtues, or Accomplishments
    ___ Used Examples to Show Each Attribute
    ___ Shared Interesting Details
    ___ Showed Impact on Your Life or Others

___ Expression & Delivery
    ___ Displayed Enthusiasm or Passion & Animation
    ___ Used Proper Tone – Honor, Sorrow, Congratulations
    ___ Used Descriptive Language, Repetition, or Other Rhythmic Devices
    ___ Sustained Eye Contact with Audience
    ___ Delivered Extemporaneously (not read) & Conversationally
    ___ Used Gestures, Professional Posture, Avoided Distractions

___ Conclusion
    ___ Used a Signal word
    ___ Summarized Attributes, Virtues, Accomplishments
    ___ Concluded with Lasting Benefits, Meaningful Sentiment or Memorable Ending

___ Time & Outline
    ___ Used Completed & Brief Outline
    ___ Stayed within Time Limit

_____ **Total Points**

# Chapter 6 – Ceremonial Speaking

Public Speaking Student Workbook

## *INSTRUCTOR EVALUATION FORM – CEREMONIAL SPEECH*

_____ TOTAL PERCENTAGE (%) POINTS   _____ GRADE

NAME: _____ DATE: _____
TOPIC: _____ TIME: _____
Outline Handed in on Time:

KEY: Excellent (5 ++)   Good (4 +)   Fair (3 ✓)   Weak (1 or 2 ✓--)   Excluded (0)

### SPEECH OUTLINE & PREPARATION - 20 (%) POINTS
__ Preparation Outline formatted (_formal format, _sections labeled, _indented, _full sentences, _transitions)
__ Preparation Outline completed (_detailed points, _citations, _References)
__ Speaking Outline Note Cards completed and used (_large cards, _dark print, _brief notes)
__ Audience Adaptation (_chose appropriate subject, _adapted speech to audience)

### INTRODUCTION - 15 (%) POINTS
__ Gained interest of audience (_motivated audience to listen)
__ Established your credibility (_how you are related to the topic)
__ Fully introduced topic (_described the purpose--e.g., tribute, eulogy, award)

### BODY = ORGANIZATION, DEVELOPMENT, & TRANSITIONS - 25 (%) POINTS
__ Effective organizational pattern (_ideas arranged logically & required sources cited)
__ Explained background and/or accomplishments (_history or contributions described)
__ Used vivid examples or personal stories to illustrate points (_highlighted reasons for tribute)
__ Values or principles (_described principles or morals to be learned from subject)
__ Smooth connectives between main points (_used signal words, _used transitions as needed)

### PRESENTATION & DELIVERY - 25 (%) POINTS
__ Strong eye contact (_looked at all areas of the room, _looked only occasionally at notes, _eye contact was sustained throughout speech, _preparation & practice were evident)
__ Effective use of voice (_conversational, _used vocal variety, _used appropriate vocal rate, _projected voice, _paused effectively, few uhms, _used correct pronunciation)
__ Expressive & Sincere (_sounded sincere, enthusiastic, or passionate)
__ Used appropriate, audience-inclusive language (_used language free of slang and profanity)
__ Effective facial expression, gestures, & animation (_used appropriate movement--not stiff or pacing, _avoided distractions--no swaying, no gum chewing, _used natural hand gestures)

### CONCLUSION & TIMING - 15 (%) POINTS
__ Ended with appropriate sentiment (_praise, admiration, sorrow, etc.)
__ Used interesting ending (_quote, anecdote, or final statement, _Invited applause)
__ Adherence to time limit (_filled time requirement--not too short or too long)

### COMMENTS:

# Chapter 6 – Ceremonial Speaking

Public Speaking Student Workbook

## SELF-EVALUATION FORM FOR THE CEREMONIAL SPEECH

NAME_____CLASS TIME_____

**OBJECTIVES**:
1. To critically evaluate your own presentation.

2. To set goals to work on for your next speech in order to improve your presentation.

**INSTRUCTIONS**:
View your recording one or more times. Use this evaluation form to analyze and evaluate the strengths and areas for improvement in your presentation.

Type of Commemorative or Ceremonial Speech (circle one):
___Toast
___Eulogy
___Tribute to a person or group of people
___Tribute to an institution or idea
___Presentation
___Acceptance
___Introduction

1. **INTRODUCTION** (Gained Attention of Audience, Described Purpose, Established Credibility—Your Relationship to Subject):

    Strengths:


    Areas for Improvement:


2. **BODY** (Used Vivid Examples with personal connection to topic, interesting details, and showed virtues/accomplishments or Noted Principles to be Learned)

    Strengths:


    Areas for Improvement:

3. **EXPRESSION** (Enthusiasm for topic & proper tone — passion, enthusiasm, personal interest in topic, respect, honor, sorrow/grief, congratulations, best wishes)

   Strengths:

   Areas for Improvement:

4. **DELIVERY** (Eye Contact, Extemporaneous — not memorized or read, & conversational):

   Strengths:

   Areas for Improvement:

5. **CONCLUSION** (Ended with Appropriate Sentiment, Used Interesting Ending, Invited Applause, when appropriate)

   Strengths:

   Areas for Improvement:

**OVERALL EVALUATION**

6. Were you Audience-Centered and Sincere? Explain.

7. Were you satisfied or happy with your speech overall? Explain.

8. What would you do differently if you could give your speech again?

Public Speaking Student Workbook

*GROUP CEREMONIAL SPEAKING ASSIGNMENT*

**SPEECH DUE DATE**:
**OUTLINE DUE DATE**:
**TIME LIMIT**:

**OBJECTIVES**:
1. To practice planning and delivering a ceremonial speech.
2. To work with other students in the class and thus continue to promote a supportive class atmosphere.

**INSTRUCTIONS**:
Form a speech team of 3 students. Together choose an award for the theme of your group. Next, choose one of the following roles: 1) The Introducer who delivers a speech of introduction for the presenter, 2) The Presenter who delivers a speech of presentation to the award recipient, 3) The Recipient who delivers a speech of acceptance. Make sure you follow the guidelines for each type of ceremonial speech (see pages 108-111). Each student will be expected to speak for at least ____ minutes. Each of you will need to complete your own outline that will be collected on the day before all speeches begin.

**EXPECTATIONS & EVALUATION CRITERIA**:

1. Plan and prepare the ceremonial speech so that each person has an equal responsibility for a part. Be sure to use examples and quotations for supporting material from at least three (3) sources.

2. Each person may use two note cards (5" x 8") for writing down key words to jog the memory while delivering the speech. Practice your speech with your cards several times so you know it well, know it fits the time requirements, and can deliver it extemporaneously.

3. Your group will come to the front of the room on the day of the class presentations. One at a time, you will step forward and present your part.

4. On the day of your presentation, you should bring an audio (video) cassette (labeled with your name) to class. After class, pick up your cassette and do a self-evaluation of your presentation. Your self-evaluation is due the class period after the last round of speeches.

5. You will receive _____ points for actively participating in the planning and delivering of your part in ceremonial speech. Evaluation criteria include: Introduction, Use of the Examples and Quotations, Use of Transitions, Content Development, Use of Vivid Language, Conclusion, Delivery (eye contact & enthusiasm), Time Limit, Audience-centeredness, and Outlines.

# Chapter 6 – Ceremonial Speaking

Public Speaking Student Workbook

## *INSTRUCTOR GROUP CEREMONIAL SPEECH EVALUATION FORM*

_____TOTAL POINTS _____PERCENTAGE (%)_____GRADE

NAME: _____ DATE: _____
TOPIC: _____ TIME: _____

KEY: Excellent (5)  Good (4 +)  Fair (3 ✓)  Weak (1 or 2 ✓--)  Excluded (0)

### SPEECH OUTLINE
__Preparation Outline formatted: ___complete, ___neat & readable
__Speaking Outline completed: ___large cards, ___dark print, ___brief notes

### ORGANIZATION, DEVELOPMENT, & TIMING
Introducer:
   ___Gained interest of audience with example, metaphor or quotation
   ___Mentioned occasion & connection to subject
   ___Included points with biographical information of achievements & contributions
   ___Welcomed speaker, used full name with title, & invited applause

Presenter:
   ___Gained interest of audience with example, metaphor or quotation
   ___Explained purpose and history of award plus why it is given
   ___Explained significance of award
   ___Mentioned your connection to the award
   ___Used descriptive language to highlight character qualities and acts of recipient
   ___Congratulated recipient, used full name with title, & name of award, invited applause

Recipient:
   ___Accepted with grace & humility
   ___Expressed gratitude for award & awareness of award's deeper meaning
   ___Thanked those who made the award possible
   ___Included vivid examples or personal stories to illustrate the meaning of the award
   ___Concluded with memorable statement /example about award, organization or event

### PRESENTATION & DELIVERY
__Showed Enthusiasm: ___Sounded Passionate
__Maintained Eye Contact: __Looked at All Areas, __Looked Only Occasionally at Notes
__Effective Use of Voice: __Sounded Conversational, __Used Vocal Variety,
   __Projected Voice So All Could Hear, ___Paused Effectively with Few Uhms
__Used Appropriate Language: __Used Stylistic Device, __Free of Slang & Profanity
__Used Effective Gestures, & Animation: __Used Appropriate Movement--Not Stiff or Pacing,
   __Avoided Distractions--Little Swaying, No Gum Chewing, __Used Natural Hand Gestures

### COMMENTS:

# Chapter 6 – Ceremonial Speaking

# 7
# Worksheets & Surveys

ULTIMATE FEARS

REVIEW OF COPING STATEMENTS

PUBLIC SPEAKING ANXIETY DIMENSIONS SURVEY

FINAL PRCA

MYSELF AS COMMUNICATOR PAPER #2

Chapter 7 – Worksheets & Surveys

## *CREATING AN ULTIMATE FEARS LIST, PART 1*

**Objectives**:

1. To discover or recognize the fears you have about speaking in public.

2. To share your biggest fears about speaking in public with another person in class.

3. To develop coping strategies to help you rationally <u>dispute</u> your fears and <u>replace</u> them with positive coping statements.

**Instructions**:

Consider a time in the past when you had to deliver a speech or speak in front of a group of people. Using the space below, list at least 5 of your biggest fears or worries about speaking in front of others.

### ULTIMATE FEARS LIST

**Fear #1**: _____

_____

**Fear #2**: _____

_____

**Fear #3**: _____

_____

**Fear #4**: _____

_____

**Fear #5**: _____

_____

**Additional Fears**: _____

_____

## CREATING AN ULTIMATE FEARS MASTER LIST, PART 2

## ULTIMATE FEARS ABOUT SPEAKING IN PUBLIC MASTER LIST

Choose a partner (or small group) and share your "Ultimate Fears List" with your fellow student(s). Together, make a master list of "Ultimate Fears about Speaking in Public."

**Fear #1**: _____

_____

**Fear #2**: _____

_____

**Fear #3**: _____

_____

**Fear #4**: _____

_____

**Fear #5**: _____

_____

**Fear #6**: _____

_____

**Fear #7**: _____

_____

**Fear #8**: _____

_____

**Fear #9**: _____

_____

Chapter 7 – Worksheets & Surveys

## *CREATING COPING STATEMENTS FOR ULTIMATE FEARS, PART 3*

Working with your fellow students in a dyad or small group, fill out the chart below about your public speaking fears, distortions, and coping statements.

### ULTIMATE FEARS & COPING STATEMENTS CHART

| YOUR FEARS<br>Irrational Beliefs & Negative Self Talk<br>(Use your master list.) | DISTORTION TERM<br>or irrational conclusion &<br>*WHY IT IS NOT TRUE | POSITIVE COPING STATEMENTS<br>(to replace your fears) |
|---|---|---|
| EXAMPLE: "Once I forgot an important point. I worry I will go always go blank and forget something." | EXAMPLE: Always-and-Never Thinking<br>*The past does not predict the future. | EXAMPLE: If I forget something, my audience friends will wait while I refer to my notes. |
| 1. | 1. | 1. |
| 2. | 2. | 2. |
| 3. | 3. | 3. |
| 4. | 4. | 4. |
| 5. | 5. | 5. |

## REVIEW OF MEMORIZED COPING STATEMENTS

1. In column one, list each of your fears and negative self-talk about public speaking.
2. In column two, list the distortion term for that fear and why it is not true.
3. In column three, write a coping statement that you memorized to replace that fearful thought.

| YOUR FEARS<br>Irrational Beliefs & Negative Self Talk | DISTORTION TERM<br>Irrational conclusion & *WHY IT IS NOT TRUE | POSITIVE COPING (replacement) STATEMENTS |
|---|---|---|
| EXAMPLE: "Once I forgot an important point. I worry I will go always go blank and forget something." | EXAMPLE: Always-and-Never Thinking *The past does not predict the future. | EXAMPLE: If I forget something, my audience friends will wait while I refer to my notes. |
| 1. | 1. | 1. |
| 2. | 2. | 2. |
| 3. | 3. | 1.  3. |

Chapter 7 – Worksheets & Surveys

## PUBLIC SPEAKING ANXIETY DIMENSIONS SURVEY*

NAME: _____ DATE: _____

In the space next to each of the following items, please write down the number that most accurately reflects your opinion.

| Strongly Disagree 1 | Moderately Disagree 2 | Slightly Disagree 3 | Neutral 4 | Slightly Agree 5 | Moderately Agree 6 | Strongly Agree 7 |
|---|---|---|---|---|---|---|

___1.   I usually think things out before I act on them.
___2.   I think more in pictures than in words.
___3.   I pay a lot of attention to my emotions or feelings when making a decision.
___4.   I do NOT have a general stress reduction plan in my life.
___5.   I can clearly visualize myself (form clear mental images) in the activities I do.
___6.   In general, I do NOT get sufficient rest or sleep.
___7.   I have few skills, if any, necessary for effective public speaking.
___8.   I avoid public speaking because I lack communication skills.
___9.   On a regular basis, I get very little physical exercise.
___10.  When I am asked to give a speech, the first thing that happens is my thoughts fill with worries about the speech and/or what could go wrong.
___11.  When I am asked to give a speech, the first thing that happens is I visually imagine what the situation would be like and/or what could go wrong.
___12.  When I am stressed, I often turn to drugs or alcohol for relief.
___13.  I am acutely aware of any physical sensations in my body before I give a speech.
___14.  I can feel even the slightest nervous sensations in my body when I'm speaking in public.
___15.  I have a lot of worrisome thoughts about giving a speech.
___16.  I am acutely aware of my bodily sensations during a public speech.
___17.  I easily form vivid pictures in my imagination about many circumstances.
___18.  I am deeply and emotionally affected by my experiences.
___19.  Most of the time, I thoroughly reason things out.
___20.  The first thing I must do to become an effective speaker is to learn public speaking skills.
___21.  Images come to my mind, often before words do.
___22.  I should take better care of my body with regular exercise and sufficient rest.
___23.  When I am asked to a give speech, the first thing that happens is I run from the situation.
___24.  Fearful emotions often overtake me when I have to give a speech or speak in public.
___25.  I notice even the slightest sensation in my body almost immediately when it begins.
___26.  My emotions can inhibit me and keep me from doing things, like giving a speech.
___27.  When I am asked to give a speech, negative thoughts immediately come to my mind.
___28.  When I am asked to give a speech, the first thing that happens is fear/anxiety grips my emotions.
___29.  I often procrastinate when assigned a project, like giving a speech.
___30.  When I am asked to give a speech, the first thing that happens is I feel some sensations in my body, such as a racing or pounding heart, nausea or stomach tightness, blushing face, rising blood pressure, or trembling hands/feet.

*The survey is from the book: *IConquer Speech Anxiety* by Karen Kangas Dwyer, 2020. KLD Books.

Public Speaking Student Workbook

## SCORING THE PUBLIC SPEAKING ANXIETY DIMENSIONS SURVEY

NAME: _____ DATE: _____

To compute your scores merely add your scores for each item as indicated below.

Dimension:                Scoring Formula:

BEHAVIOR (B):        Add   7 __, 8 __, 20__, 23__, 29__ =  TOTAL_____

AFFECT (A):             Add   3 __, 18 __, 24__, 26__, 28__ =  TOTAL_____

SENSATIONS (S):     Add   13 __, 14 __, 16__, 25__, 30__ =  TOTAL_____

IMAGERY (I):           Add   2 __, 5 __, 11__, 17__, 21__ =  TOTAL_____

COGNITION (C):      Add   1 __, 10 __, 15__, 19__, 27__ =  TOTAL_____

STRESS (S):              Add   4 __, 6 __, 9 __, 12__, 22__ =  TOTAL_____
(DRUGS & BIOLOGICAL)


1. My highest score is in the following dimension _____

2. My second highest score is in the following dimension _____

3. My third highest score is in the following dimension _____

4. According to this survey, my Firing Order of dimensions is _____

5. Before this survey, I determined my Firing Order of dimensions to be _____

Chapter 7 – Worksheets & Surveys

## MATCHING TREATMENT TO THE DIMENSION SCORES

Each dimension score can range from five (5) to thirty-five (30). Now list your scores from the highest dimension score to the lowest dimension score using the chart below.

|    | DIMENSION | SURVEY SCORE | TECHNIQUE |
|----|-----------|--------------|-----------|
| 1. |           |              |           |
| 2. |           |              |           |
| 3. |           |              |           |
| 4. |           |              |           |
| 5. |           |              |           |
| 6. |           |              |           |
| 7. |           |              |           |

**Star* the top three dimensions of your Firing Order.**

Using the following list of personality dimensions with techniques that target those specific dimensions, complete the chart with the techniques that are most appropriate for your dimensions.

**Personality Dimension     Anxiety Reduction Technique**

1. Behavior Dimension: Skills Training (enroll in a public speaking class or workshop where you can learn and practice public speaking skills).

2. Affect Dimension: Systematic Desensitization and Diaphragmatic Breathing

3. Sensation Dimension: Systematic Desensitization and Diaphragmatic Breathing

4. Imagery Dimension: Systematic Desensitization and/or Mental Rehearsal

5. Cognitive Dimension: Cognitive Restructuring and/or Mental Rehearsal.

6. Stress/ Biological Dimension: Physical Exercise, Diaphragmatic Breathing, and Stress-reduction plans (always in cooperation with a physician).

Public Speaking Student Workbook

*THE SPEECH CONSULTING SURVEY*

1. How many times did visit the Speech Center with your class? _____

2. How many times did you visit the Speech Center on your own? _____

3. Why did you choose to visit the Speech Center on your own?

4. How helpful was the Speech Center for you (circle one)?

    Very Helpful    Helpful    Undecided    Not Helpful    Not Helpful at All

5. List below any suggestions you have for the Speech Center.

## HOW I HAVE CHANGED OVER THE SEMESTER

6. Please review your communication apprehension assessment scores on the next page. Compare these final scores with your initial scores on Workbook p. 15. Then describe how your anxiety levels have changed over the semester.

Chapter 7 – Worksheets & Surveys

*FINAL ASSESSMENT OF YOUR COMMUNICATION APPREHENSION LEVEL*

Name:_____   Date:_____

**McCroskey's Personal Report of Communication Apprehension - PRCA-24\***

Directions: This instrument is composed of twenty-four statements concerning feelings about communicating with others. Work quickly, record your first impression. Please indicate in the space provided the degree to which each statement applies to you by marking:

(1) STRONGLY AGREE  (2) AGREE  (3) ARE UNDECIDED  (4) DISAGREE  (5) STRONGLY DISAGREE

____   1. I dislike participating in group discussions.
____   2. Generally, I am comfortable while participating in group discussions.
____   3. I am tense and nervous while participating in group discussions.
____   4. I like to get involved in group discussions.
____   5. Engaging in a group discussion with new people makes me tense and nervous.
____   6. I am calm and relaxed while participating in group discussions.
____   7. Generally, I am nervous when I have to participate in a meeting.
____   8. Usually, I am calm and relaxed while participating in a meeting.
____   9. I am very calm and relaxed when I am called upon to express an opinion at a meeting.
____   10. I am afraid to express myself at meetings.
____   11. Communicating at meetings usually makes me uncomfortable.
____   12. I am very relaxed when answering questions at a meeting.
____   13. While participating in a conversation with a new acquaintance, I feel very nervous.
____   14. I have no fear of speaking up in conversations.
____   15. Ordinarily I am very tense and nervous in conversations.
____   16. Ordinarily I am very calm and relaxed in conversations.
____   17. While conversing with a new acquaintance, I feel very relaxed.
____   18. I'm afraid to speak up in conversations.
____   19. I have no fear of giving a speech.
____   20. Certain parts of my body feel very tense and rigid while I am giving a speech.
____   21. I feel relaxed while giving a speech.
____   22. My thoughts become confused and jumbled when I am giving a speech.
____   23. I face the prospect of giving a speech with confidence.
____   24. While giving a speech, I get so nervous I forget facts I really know.

Public Speaking Student Workbook

## *SCORING AND INTERPRETING YOUR SCORES*

**SCORING: Compute your scores by adding or subtracting your scores for each item.**

Name:_____ ID#:_____ Date:_____

<u>Subscore (Context)</u>   <u>Scoring Formula</u>

**Group Discussions:** 18 plus + scores for items 2____, 4____, & 6____; minus (-) scores for items 1____, 3____, & 5____ = _____.

**Meetings:** 18 plus + scores for items 8____, 9____, & 12____; minus (-) scores for items 7____, 10____, & 11____ = _____.

**Interpersonal Conversations:** 18 plus + scores for items 14____, 16____, & 17____; minus(-) scores for items 13____, 15____, & 18____ = _____.

**Public Speaking:** 18 plus+ scores for items 19____, 21____, & 23____; minus (-) scores for items 20____, 22____, & 24____ = _____.

**Overall:** Add all four subscores together (Group Discussions + Meetings + Interpersonal Conversations + Public Speaking)= _____.

<u>COMPUTE your five scores</u> above and write them in the following chart under <u>YOUR SCORE</u>.

### YOUR PRCA SCORES CHART

| <u>OVERALL & CONTEXT</u> | <u>YOUR SCORE</u> | "" CHECK YOUR LEVEL / RANGE  LOW   AVERAGE   HIGH |
|---|---|---|
| Group | _____ | ____  ____  ____ |
| Meetings | _____ | ____  ____  ____ |
| Interpersonal | _____ | ____  ____  ____ |
| Public Speaking | _____ | ____  ____  ____ |
| Overall | _____ | |

<u>To interpret your score</u>, compare your scores with those who have completed the PRCA-24.

### NORMS CHART FOR THE PRCA-24

| CONTEXT & OVERALL | AVERAGE SCORE | AVERAGE RANGE | HIGH CA SCORES |
|---|---|---|---|
| <u>Group</u> | <u>15.4</u> | <u>11 to 20</u> | <u>21 & ABOVE</u> |
| <u>Meeting</u> | <u>16.4</u> | <u>12 to 21</u> | <u>22 & ABOVE</u> |
| <u>Interpersonal</u> | <u>14.5</u> | <u>10 to 18</u> | <u>19 & ABOVE</u> |
| <u>Public Speaking</u> | <u>19.3</u> | <u>14 to 24</u> | <u>25 & ABOVE</u> |
| <u>Overall</u> | <u>65.6</u> | <u>50 to 80</u> | <u>81 & ABOVE</u> |

Public Speaking Student Workbook

## *MYSELF AS A COMMUNICATOR PAPER #2*

1. Please describe how you see yourself as a "communicator" NOW in the following situations:

    a. In Everyday Conversations:

    b. In Class or Group Discussions:

    c. In Meetings:

    d. In Public Speaking:

    e. Overall (in most situations):

### ASSESSING THE CHANGE IN YOUR ANXIETY LEVEL

2. Please review how you described yourself as a communicator during the first week of class in your *Myself as a Communicator Paper #1* (see Workbook page 10 and your journal). Then, describe changes or improvements based upon what you wrote THEN and NOW.

3. Please list the "overcoming speech fright" techniques that were helpful to you in this course. Please star* the technique that was most helpful in reducing your speech anxiety.

4. Please list the firing order of dimensions involved in your speech anxiety.

ADDITIONAL COMMENTS

# 8

# Peer Feedback Forms

### FOR

### ALL SPEECHES

# Chapter 8 – Peer Feedback Forms

## *PEER FEEDBACK INSTRUCTIONS*

**OBJECTIVES**:
1. To learn public speaking principles by observing other speakers.
2. To practice critical listening.
3. To analyze the speeches of fellow students in order to improve your own speaking abilities.
4. To critique the speeches of fellow students in order to offer them your concern and feedback (including both positive comments and suggestions for improvement).

**INSTRUCTIONS**:
For each speech round, your instructor will ask you to fill out peer speech feedback forms on some of your fellow students. You will critically listen to each speaker, fill in the peer feedback forms with comments, and turn the forms in at the end of the class period. You will receive points for doing the evaluations, but most importantly the speakers will receive feedback from caring listeners. In addition, you will be able to practice critical listening and further learn effective principles of public speaking.

**REQUIREMENTS & EVALUATION CRITERIA**:
1. Bring this workbook to class so you will have the feedback forms at hand.

2. There are eight feedback forms per speech round so you can evaluate up to eight speeches per round with the forms provided. Carefully, tear out each sheet on the perforated line.

3. Evaluate each important aspect of public speaking using the suggested key of symbols or numbers. Also make specific comments beside each section, as well as in response to the final questions on back of each form.

4. In your comments, follow these tips:
   a. PLEASE SAY SOMETHING POSITIVE (where has the speaker improved or what did he/she do well);
   b. PLEASE SAY SOMETHING SPECIFIC (Explain what you thought was effective. "I thought your speech was great!" is NOT specific. Also, please do NOT say things like "You look cute today" or "I like your shirt.");
   c. PLEASE SAY SOMETHING CONSTRUCTIVE (Tell the speaker what you think could make the speech even better. For example, you might write, "Try telling us about your personal example in the introduction instead of the conclusion because it would add to your credibility during the speech."); and
   d. PLEASE USE FIRST PERSON IN YOUR SUGGESTIONS (It is more supportive to say, "I would like to see you use more expert quotations" than to say, "You should use more quotations.")

   5. You will receive____ points for completing each peer feedback form or round of peer feedback forms.

# Public Speaking Student Workbook
## Peer Feedback Form — Informative Speech #1

Speaker _____ Topic _____ Evaluator _____

*Instructions for this form:*
- Mark items using this system:

| Excellent = plus (+) | Average = check (✓) | Needs Improvement = circle the item |
|---|---|---|

- Write comments that will help the speaker, following this acronym:
    **S**pecific (For example, not "Good job" but "Excellent attention getter!")
    **H**elpful (Give ideas in a helpful way. Use "I" statements — "I'd like to see a visual aid.")
    **I**deas (Write down 3-4 ideas for improvement for this speech)
    **P**raise (Write down 3-4 things the speaker did well in this speech)

*Introduction*
__Grabbed attention __Revealed topic __Motivated audience __Established credibility
__Previewed main points

*Body*
__Clear main points __Easy to follow __Used clear transitions __Clear explanation of process
__Adapted to audience

*Visual Aids*
__Easy to read __Impactful __ text minimal, __simple theme, __powerful images,
   __large fonts, __looked at computer display NOT the screen

*Delivery*
__Eye contact __Sounded conversational __Gestures __Used effective pauses __Avoided
       vocal fillers (uh, uhms) __Used appropriate language __Avoided distractions

*Conclusion*
__Signaled ending __Summarized main points __Motivated audience __Memorable ending

*Overall Speech Rating*
Choose one: __Excellent __Very Good __Good __Average __Needs Improvement

What about this speech did you appreciate?

What suggestions for improvement would you give?

# Chapter 8 – Peer Feedback Forms

# Public Speaking Student Workbook
## *Peer Feedback Form — Informative Speech #1*

Speaker _____ Topic _____ Evaluator _____

*Instructions for this form*:
- Mark items using this system:

| Excellent = plus (+) | Average = check (✓) | Needs Improvement = circle the item |

- Write comments that will help the speaker, following this acronym:
    **S**pecific (For example, not "Good job" but "Excellent attention getter!")
    **H**elpful (Give ideas in a helpful way. Use "I" statements — "I'd like to see a visual aid.")
    **I**deas (Write down 3-4 ideas for improvement for this speech)
    **P**raise (Write down 3-4 things the speaker did well in this speech)

*Introduction*
__Grabbed attention __Revealed topic __Motivated audience __Established credibility
__Previewed main points

*Body*
__Clear main points __Easy to follow __Used clear transitions __Clear explanation of process
__Adapted to audience

*Presentational Slides*
__Easy to read __Impactful __ text minimal, __simple theme, __powerful images,
    __large fonts, __looked at computer display NOT the screen

*Delivery*
__Eye contact __Sounded conversational __Gestures __Used effective pauses __Avoided
    vocal fillers (uh, uhms) __Used appropriate language __Avoided distractions

*Conclusion*
__Signaled ending __Summarized main points __Motivated audience __Memorable ending

*Overall Speech Rating*
Choose one: ___Excellent ___Very Good ___Good ___Average ___Needs Improvement

What about this speech did you appreciate?

What suggestions for improvement would you give?

# Chapter 8 – Peer Feedback Forms

# Public Speaking Student Workbook
## *Peer Feedback Form — Informative Speech #1*

Speaker _____ Topic _____ Evaluator _____

*Instructions for this form:*
- Mark items using this system:

| Excellent = plus (+) | Average = check (✓) | Needs Improvement = circle the item |
|---|---|---|

- Write comments that will help the speaker, following this acronym:
  **S**pecific (For example, not "Good job" but "Excellent attention getter!")
  **H**elpful (Give ideas in a helpful way. Use "I" statements — "I'd like to see a visual aid.")
  **I**deas (Write down 3-4 ideas for improvement for this speech)
  **P**raise (Write down 3-4 things the speaker did well in this speech)

*Introduction*
__Grabbed attention __Revealed topic __Motivated audience __Established credibility
__Previewed main points

*Body*
__Clear main points __Easy to follow __Used clear transitions __Clear explanation of process
__Adapted to audience

*Presentational Slides*
__Easy to read __Impactful __ text minimal, __simple theme, __powerful images,
  __large fonts, __looked at computer display NOT the screen

*Delivery*
__Eye contact __Sounded conversational __Gestures __Used effective pauses __Avoided
  vocal fillers (uh, uhms) __Used appropriate language __Avoided distractions

*Conclusion*
__Signaled ending __Summarized main points __Motivated audience __Memorable ending

*Overall Speech Rating*
Choose one: ___Excellent ___Very Good ___Good ___Average ___Needs Improvement

What about this speech did you appreciate?

What suggestions for improvement would you give?

# Chapter 8 – Peer Feedback Forms

# Public Speaking Student Workbook
## *Peer Feedback Form—Informative Speech #1*

Speaker _____ Topic _____ Evaluator _____

*Instructions for this form*:
- Mark items using this system:

| Excellent = plus (+) | Average = check (✓) | Needs Improvement = circle the item |
|---|---|---|

- Write comments that will help the speaker, following this acronym:
    **S**pecific (For example, not "Good job" but "Excellent attention getter!")
    **H**elpful (Give ideas in a helpful way. Use "I" statements—"I'd like to see a visual aid.")
    **I**deas (Write down 3-4 ideas for improvement for this speech)
    **P**raise (Write down 3-4 things the speaker did well in this speech)

*Introduction*
__Grabbed attention __Revealed topic __Motivated audience __Established credibility
__Previewed main points

*Body*
__Clear main points __Easy to follow __Used clear transitions __Clear explanation of process
__Adapted to audience

*Presentational Slides*
__Easy to read __Impactful __ text minimal, __simple theme, __powerful images,
   __large fonts, __looked at computer display NOT the screen

*Delivery*
__Eye contact __Sounded conversational __Gestures __Used effective pauses __Avoided
       vocal fillers (uh, uhms) __Used appropriate language __Avoided distractions

*Conclusion*
__Signaled ending __Summarized main points __Motivated audience __Memorable ending

*Overall Speech Rating*
Choose one: ___Excellent ___Very Good ___Good ___Average ___Needs Improvement

What about this speech did you appreciate?

What suggestions for improvement would you give?

# Chapter 8 – Peer Feedback Forms

# Public Speaking Student Workbook
## *Peer Feedback Form — Informative Speech #1*

Speaker _____ Topic _____ Evaluator _____

*Instructions for this form*:
- Mark items using this system:

| Excellent = plus (+) | Average = check (✓) | Needs Improvement = circle the item |
|---|---|---|

- Write comments that will help the speaker, following this acronym:
    **S**pecific (For example, not "Good job" but "Excellent attention getter!")
    **H**elpful (Give ideas in a helpful way. Use "I" statements — "I'd like to see a visual aid.")
    **I**deas (Write down 3-4 ideas for improvement for this speech)
    **P**raise (Write down 3-4 things the speaker did well in this speech)

*Introduction*
__Grabbed attention __Revealed topic __Motivated audience __Established credibility
__Previewed main points

*Body*
__Clear main points __Easy to follow __Used clear transitions __Clear explanation of process
__Adapted to audience

*Presentational Slides*
__Easy to read __Impactful __ text minimal, __simple theme, __powerful images,
    __large fonts, __looked at computer display NOT the screen

*Delivery*
__Eye contact __Sounded conversational __Gestures __Used effective pauses __Avoided
    vocal fillers (uh, uhms) __Used appropriate language __Avoided distractions

*Conclusion*
__Signaled ending __Summarized main points __Motivated audience __Memorable ending

*Overall Speech Rating*
Choose one: ___Excellent ___Very Good ___Good ___Average ___Needs Improvement

What about this speech did you appreciate?

What suggestions for improvement would you give?

# Chapter 8 – Peer Feedback Forms

# Public Speaking Student Workbook
## *Peer Feedback Form – Informative Speech #1*

Speaker _____ Topic _____ Evaluator _____

*Instructions for this form*:
- Mark items using this system:

| Excellent = plus (+) | Average = check (✓) | Needs Improvement = circle the item |

- Write comments that will help the speaker, following this acronym:
    **S**pecific (For example, not "Good job" but "Excellent attention getter!")
    **H**elpful (Give ideas in a helpful way. Use "I" statements – "I'd like to see a visual aid.")
    **I**deas (Write down 3-4 ideas for improvement for this speech)
    **P**raise (Write down 3-4 things the speaker did well in this speech)

*Introduction*
__Grabbed attention __Revealed topic __Motivated audience __Established credibility
__Previewed main points

*Body*
__Clear main points __Easy to follow __Used clear transitions __Clear explanation of process
__Adapted to audience

*Presentational Slides*
__Easy to read __Impactful __ text minimal, __simple theme, __powerful images,
   __large fonts, __looked at computer display NOT the screen

*Delivery*
__Eye contact __Sounded conversational __Gestures __Used effective pauses __Avoided
     vocal fillers (uh, uhms) __Used appropriate language __Avoided distractions

*Conclusion*
__Signaled ending __Summarized main points __Motivated audience __Memorable ending

*Overall Speech Rating*
Choose one: __Excellent __Very Good __Good __Average __Needs Improvement

What about this speech did you appreciate?

What suggestions for improvement would you give?

# Chapter 8 – Peer Feedback Forms

# Public Speaking Student Workbook
## *Peer Feedback Form — Informative Speech #1*

Speaker _____ Topic _____ Evaluator _____

*Instructions for this form*:
- Mark items using this system:

  | Excellent = plus (+) | Average = check (✓) | Needs Improvement = circle the item |
  |---|---|---|

- Write comments that will help the speaker, following this acronym:
    **S**pecific (For example, not "Good job" but "Excellent attention getter!")
    **H**elpful (Give ideas in a helpful way. Use "I" statements — "I'd like to see a visual aid.")
    **I**deas (Write down 3-4 ideas for improvement for this speech)
    **P**raise (Write down 3-4 things the speaker did well in this speech)

*Introduction*
__Grabbed attention __Revealed topic __Motivated audience __Established credibility
__Previewed main points

*Body*
__Clear main points __Easy to follow __Used clear transitions __Clear explanation of process
__Adapted to audience

*Presentational Slides*
__Easy to read __Impactful __ text minimal, __simple theme, __powerful images,
  __large fonts, __looked at computer display NOT the screen

*Delivery*
__Eye contact __Sounded conversational __Gestures __Used effective pauses __Avoided
    vocal fillers (uh, uhms) __Used appropriate language __Avoided distractions

*Conclusion*
__Signaled ending __Summarized main points __Motivated audience __Memorable ending

*Overall Speech Rating*
Choose one: ___Excellent ___Very Good ___Good ___Average ___Needs Improvement

What about this speech did you appreciate?

What suggestions for improvement would you give?

# Chapter 8 – Peer Feedback Forms

# Public Speaking Student Workbook
## *Peer Feedback Form — Informative Speech #1*

Speaker _____ Topic _____ Evaluator _____

*Instructions for this form*:
- Mark items using this system:

| Excellent = plus (+) | Average = check (✓) | Needs Improvement = circle the item |

- Write comments that will help the speaker, following this acronym:
    **S**pecific (For example, not "Good job" but "Excellent attention getter!")
    **H**elpful (Give ideas in a helpful way. Use "I" statements — "I'd like to see a visual aid.")
    **I**deas (Write down 3-4 ideas for improvement for this speech)
    **P**raise (Write down 3-4 things the speaker did well in this speech)

*Introduction*
__Grabbed attention __Revealed topic __Motivated audience __Established credibility
__Previewed main points

*Body*
__Clear main points __Easy to follow __Used clear transitions __Clear explanation of process
__Adapted to audience

*Presentational Slides*
__Easy to read __Impactful __ text minimal, __simple theme, __powerful images,
    __large fonts, __looked at computer display NOT the screen

*Delivery*
__Eye contact __Sounded conversational __Gestures __Used effective pauses __Avoided
    vocal fillers (uh, uhms) __Used appropriate language __Avoided distractions

*Conclusion*
__Signaled ending __Summarized main points __Motivated audience __Memorable ending

*Overall Speech Rating*
Choose one: ___Excellent ___Very Good ___Good ___Average ___Needs Improvement

What about this speech did you appreciate?

What suggestions for improvement would you give?

# Chapter 8 – Peer Feedback Forms

# Public Speaking Student Workbook
## *Peer Feedback Form — Informative Speech #2*

Speaker _____ Topic _____ Evaluator _____

*Instructions for this form:*
- Mark items using this system:

  | Excellent = plus (+) | Average = check (✓) | Needs Improvement = circle the item |
  |---|---|---|

- Write comments that will help the speaker, following this acronym:
    **S**pecific (For example, not "Good job" but "Excellent attention getter!")
    **H**elpful (Give ideas in a helpful way. Use "I" statements — "I'd like to see a visual aid.")
    **I**deas (Write down 3-4 ideas for improvement for this speech)
    **P**raise (Write down 3-4 things the speaker did well in this speech)

*Introduction*
__Grabbed attention __Revealed topic __Motivated audience __Established credibility
__Previewed main points

*Body*
__Clear main points __Easy to follow __Used clear transitions __Clear explanation of process
__Adapted to audience

*Presentational Slides*
__Easy to read __Impactful __text minimal, __simple theme, __powerful images,
  __large fonts, __looked at computer display NOT the screen

*Delivery*
__Eye contact __Sounded conversational __Gestures __Used effective pauses __Avoided
    vocal fillers (uh, uhms) __Used appropriate language __Avoided distractions

*Conclusion*
__Signaled ending __Summarized main points __Motivated audience __Memorable ending

*Overall Speech Rating*
Choose one: ___Excellent ___Very Good ___Good ___Average ___Needs Improvement

What about this speech did you appreciate?

What suggestions for improvement would you give?

# Chapter 8 – Peer Feedback Forms

# Public Speaking Student Workbook
## *Peer Feedback Form — Informative Speech #2*

Speaker _____ Topic _____ Evaluator _____

*Instructions for this form*:
- Mark items using this system:

  | Excellent = plus (+) | Average = check (✓) | Needs Improvement = circle the item |
  |---|---|---|

- Write comments that will help the speaker, following this acronym:
  **S**pecific (For example, not "Good job" but "Excellent attention getter!")
  **H**elpful (Give ideas in a helpful way. Use "I" statements — "I'd like to see a visual aid.")
  **I**deas (Write down 3-4 ideas for improvement for this speech)
  **P**raise (Write down 3-4 things the speaker did well in this speech)

*Introduction*
__Grabbed attention __Revealed topic __Motivated audience __Established credibility
__Previewed main points

*Body*
__Clear main points __Used clear transitions __Organization easy to follow
__Used sufficient supporting material __Variety of sources __Cited all supporting material
__Interesting, informative (not persuasive) topic __Adapted to audience
__Used audience analysis

*Presentational Slides*
__Easy to read __Impactful __ text minimal, __simple theme, __powerful images,
   __large fonts, __looked at computer display NOT the screen

*Delivery*
__Eye contact __Vocal variety __Used appropriate gestures __Used effective pauses
__Avoided vocal fillers (uh, uhms) __Used appropriate rate __Used creative language
__Used appropriate language __Avoided distractions

*Conclusion*
__Signaled ending __Summarized main points __Motivated audience
__Memorable ending or dramatic appeal

*Overall Speech Rating*
Choose one: ___Excellent ___Very Good ___Good ___Average ___Needs Improvement

What about this speech did you appreciate?

What suggestions for improvement would you give?

# Chapter 8 – Peer Feedback Forms

# Public Speaking Student Workbook
## *Peer Feedback Form – Informative Speech 2*

Speaker _____ Topic _____ Evaluator _____

*Instructions for this form*:
- Mark items using this system:

| Excellent = plus (+) | Average = check (✓) | Needs Improvement = circle the item |
|---|---|---|

- Write comments that will help the speaker, following this acronym:
    **S**pecific (For example, not "Good job" but "Excellent attention getter!")
    **H**elpful (Give ideas in a helpful way. Use "I" statements – "I'd like to see a visual aid.")
    **I**deas (Write down 3-4 ideas for improvement for this speech)
    **P**raise (Write down 3-4 things the speaker did well in this speech)

*Introduction*
\_\_Grabbed attention \_\_Revealed topic \_\_Motivated audience \_\_Established credibility
\_\_Previewed main points

*Body*
\_\_Clear main points \_\_Used clear transitions \_\_Organization easy to follow
\_\_Used sufficient supporting material \_\_Variety of sources \_\_Cited all supporting material
\_\_Interesting, informative (not persuasive) topic \_\_Adapted to audience
\_\_Used audience analysis

*Presentational Slides*
\_\_Easy to read \_\_Impactful \_\_ text minimal, \_\_simple theme, \_\_powerful images,
   \_\_large fonts, \_\_looked at computer display NOT the screen

*Delivery*
\_\_Eye contact \_\_Vocal variety \_\_Used appropriate gestures \_\_Used effective pauses
\_\_Avoided vocal fillers (uh, uhms) \_\_Used appropriate rate \_\_Used creative language
\_\_Used appropriate language \_\_Avoided distractions

*Conclusion*
\_\_Signaled ending \_\_Summarized main points \_\_Motivated audience
\_\_Memorable ending or dramatic appeal

*Overall Speech Rating*
Choose one: \_\_\_Excellent \_\_\_Very Good \_\_\_Good \_\_\_Average \_\_\_Needs Improvement

What about this speech did you appreciate?

What suggestions for improvement would you give?

# Chapter 8 – Peer Feedback Forms

# Public Speaking Student Workbook
## *Peer Feedback Form — Informative Speech 2*

Speaker _____ Topic _____ Evaluator _____

*Instructions for this form*:
- Mark items using this system:

| Excellent = plus (+) | Average = check (✓) | Needs Improvement = circle the item |

- Write comments that will help the speaker, following this acronym:
    **S**pecific (For example, not "Good job" but "Excellent attention getter!")
    **H**elpful (Give ideas in a helpful way. Use "I" statements — "I'd like to see a visual aid.")
    **I**deas (Write down 3-4 ideas for improvement for this speech)
    **P**raise (Write down 3-4 things the speaker did well in this speech)

*Introduction*
__Grabbed attention __Revealed topic __Motivated audience __Established credibility
__Previewed main points

*Body*
    __**Clear main points __Used clear transitions __Organization easy to follow**
__Used sufficient supporting material __Variety of sources __Cited all supporting material
__Interesting, informative (not persuasive) topic __Adapted to audience
__Used audience analysis

*Presentational Slides*
__Easy to read __Impactful __ text minimal, __simple theme, __powerful images,
    __large fonts, __looked at computer display NOT the screen

*Delivery*
__Eye contact __Vocal variety __Used appropriate gestures __Used effective pauses
__Avoided vocal fillers (uh, uhms) __Used appropriate rate __Used creative language
__Used appropriate language __Avoided distractions

*Conclusion*
__Signaled ending __Summarized main points __Motivated audience
__Memorable ending or dramatic appeal

*Overall Speech Rating*
Choose one: __Excellent __Very Good __Good __Average __Needs Improvement

What about this speech did you appreciate?

What suggestions for improvement would you give?

# Chapter 8 – Peer Feedback Forms

# Public Speaking Student Workbook
## *Peer Feedback Form — Informative Speech 2*

Speaker _____ Topic _____ Evaluator _____

*Instructions for this form:*
- Mark items using this system:

  | Excellent = plus (+) | Average = check (✓) | Needs Improvement = circle the item |

- Write comments that will help the speaker, following this acronym:
    **S**pecific (For example, not "Good job" but "Excellent attention getter!")
    **H**elpful (Give ideas in a helpful way. Use "I" statements — "I'd like to see a visual aid.")
    **I**deas (Write down 3-4 ideas for improvement for this speech)
    **P**raise (Write down 3-4 things the speaker did well in this speech)

*Introduction*
__Grabbed attention __Revealed topic __Motivated audience __Established credibility
__Previewed main points

*Body*
__Clear main points __Used clear transitions __Organization easy to follow
__Used sufficient supporting material __Variety of sources __Cited all supporting material
__Interesting, informative (not persuasive) topic __Adapted to audience
__Used audience analysis

*Presentational Slides*
__Easy to read __Impactful __ text minimal, __simple theme, __powerful images,
   __large fonts, __looked at computer display NOT the screen

*Delivery*
__Eye contact __Vocal variety __Used appropriate gestures __Used effective pauses
__Avoided vocal fillers (uh, uhms) __Used appropriate rate __Used creative language
__Used appropriate language __Avoided distractions

*Conclusion*
__Signaled ending __Summarized main points __Motivated audience
__Memorable ending or dramatic appeal

*Overall Speech Rating*
Choose one: ___Excellent ___Very Good ___Good ___Average ___Needs Improvement

What about this speech did you appreciate?

What suggestions for improvement would you give?

# Chapter 8 – Peer Feedback Forms

# Public Speaking Student Workbook
## *Peer Feedback Form — Informative Speech 2*

Speaker _____ Topic _____ Evaluator _____

*Instructions for this form*:
- Mark items using this system:

  | Excellent = plus (+) | Average = check (✓) | Needs Improvement = circle the item |

- Write comments that will help the speaker, following this acronym:
  **S**pecific (For example, not "Good job" but "Excellent attention getter!")
  **H**elpful (Give ideas in a helpful way. Use "I" statements — "I'd like to see a visual aid.")
  **I**deas (Write down 3-4 ideas for improvement for this speech)
  **P**raise (Write down 3-4 things the speaker did well in this speech)

*Introduction*
__Grabbed attention __Revealed topic __Motivated audience __Established credibility
__Previewed main points

*Body*
__Clear main points __Used clear transitions __Organization easy to follow
__Used sufficient supporting material __Variety of sources __Cited all supporting material
__Interesting, informative (not persuasive) topic __Adapted to audience
__Used audience analysis

*Presentational Slides*
__Easy to read __Impactful __ text minimal, __simple theme, __powerful images,
   __large fonts, __looked at computer display NOT the screen

*Delivery*
__Eye contact __Vocal variety __Used appropriate gestures __Used effective pauses
__Avoided vocal fillers (uh, uhms) __Used appropriate rate __Used creative language
__Used appropriate language __Avoided distractions

*Conclusion*
__Signaled ending __Summarized main points __Motivated audience
__Memorable ending or dramatic appeal

*Overall Speech Rating*
Choose one: ___Excellent ___Very Good ___Good ___Average ___Needs Improvement

What about this speech did you appreciate?
What suggestions for improvement would you give?

# Chapter 8 – Peer Feedback Forms

# Public Speaking Student Workbook
*Peer Feedback Form – Informative Speech 2*

Speaker _____ Topic _____ Evaluator _____

*Instructions for this form:*
- Mark items using this system:

  | Excellent = plus (+) | Average = check (✓) | Needs Improvement = circle the item |
  |---|---|---|

- Write comments that will help the speaker, following this acronym:
  **S**pecific (For example, not "Good job" but "Excellent attention getter!")
  **H**elpful (Give ideas in a helpful way. Use "I" statements – "I'd like to see a visual aid.")
  **I**deas (Write down 3-4 ideas for improvement for this speech)
  **P**raise (Write down 3-4 things the speaker did well in this speech)

*Introduction*
__Grabbed attention __Revealed topic __Motivated audience __Established credibility
__Previewed main points

*Body*
__Clear main points __Used clear transitions __Organization easy to follow
__Used sufficient supporting material __Variety of sources __Cited all supporting material
__Interesting, informative (not persuasive) topic __Adapted to audience
__Used audience analysis

*Presentational Slides*
__Easy to read __Impactful __ text minimal, __simple theme, __powerful images,
   __large fonts, __looked at computer display NOT the screen

*Delivery*
__Eye contact __Vocal variety __Used appropriate gestures __Used effective pauses
__Avoided vocal fillers (uh, uhms) __Used appropriate rate __Used creative language
__Used appropriate language __Avoided distractions

*Conclusion*
__Signaled ending __Summarized main points __Motivated audience
__Memorable ending or dramatic appeal

*Overall Speech Rating*
Choose one: ___Excellent ___Very Good ___Good ___Average ___Needs Improvement

What about this speech did you appreciate?

# Chapter 8 – Peer Feedback Forms

# Public Speaking Student Workbook
## *Peer Feedback Form – Informative Speech 2*

Speaker _____ Topic _____ Evaluator _____

*Instructions for this form*:
- Mark items using this system:

  | Excellent = plus (+) | Average = check (✓) | Needs Improvement = circle the item |

- Write comments that will help the speaker, following this acronym:
  **S**pecific (For example, not "Good job" but "Excellent attention getter!")
  **H**elpful (Give ideas in a helpful way. Use "I" statements – "I'd like to see a visual aid.")
  **I**deas (Write down 3-4 ideas for improvement for this speech)
  **P**raise (Write down 3-4 things the speaker did well in this speech)

*Introduction*
__Grabbed attention __Revealed topic __Motivated audience __Established credibility
__Previewed main points

*Body*
__Clear main points __Used clear transitions __Organization easy to follow
__Used sufficient supporting material __Variety of sources __Cited all supporting material
__Interesting, informative (not persuasive) topic __ Adapted to audience
__Used audience analysis

*Presentational Slides*
__Easy to read __Impactful __ text minimal, __simple theme, __powerful images,
   __large fonts, __looked at computer display NOT the screen

*Delivery*
__Eye contact __Vocal variety __Used appropriate gestures __Used effective pauses
__Avoided vocal fillers (uh, uhms) __Used appropriate rate __Used creative language
__Used appropriate language __Avoided distractions

*Conclusion*
__Signaled ending __Summarized main points __Motivated audience
__Memorable ending or dramatic appeal

*Overall Speech Rating*
Choose one: ___Excellent ___Very Good ___Good ___Average ___Needs Improvement

What about this speech did you appreciate?

What suggestions for improvement would you give?

# Chapter 8 – Peer Feedback Forms

# Public Speaking Student Workbook
## *Peer Feedback Form — Informative Speech 2*

Speaker _____ Topic _____ Evaluator _____

*Instructions for this form*:
- Mark items using this system:

| Excellent = plus (+) | Average = check (✓) | Needs Improvement = circle the item |

- Write comments that will help the speaker, following this acronym:
    **S**pecific (For example, not "Good job" but "Excellent attention getter!")
    **H**elpful (Give ideas in a helpful way. Use "I" statements — "I'd like to see a visual aid.")
    **I**deas (Write down 3-4 ideas for improvement for this speech)
    **P**raise (Write down 3-4 things the speaker did well in this speech)

*Introduction*
__Grabbed attention __Revealed topic __Motivated audience __Established credibility
__Previewed main points

*Body*
__Clear main points __Used clear transitions __Organization easy to follow
__Used sufficient supporting material __Variety of sources __Cited all supporting material
__Interesting, informative (not persuasive) topic __Adapted to audience
__Used audience analysis

*Presentational Slides*
__Easy to read __Impactful __ text minimal, __simple theme, __powerful images,
    __large fonts, __looked at computer display NOT the screen

*Delivery*
__Eye contact __Vocal variety __Used appropriate gestures __Used effective pauses
__Avoided vocal fillers (uh, uhms) __Used appropriate rate __Used creative language
__Used appropriate language __Avoided distractions

*Conclusion*
__Signaled ending __Summarized main points __Motivated audience
__Memorable ending or dramatic appeal

*Overall Speech Rating*
Choose one: ___Excellent ___Very Good ___Good ___Average ___Needs Improvement

What about this speech did you appreciate?

What suggestions for improvement would you give?

# Chapter 8 – Peer Feedback Forms

# Public Speaking Student Workbook
## *Peer Feedback Form—Informative Speech 2*

Speaker _____ Topic _____ Evaluator _____

*Instructions for this form:*
- Mark items using this system:

| Excellent = plus (+) | Average = check (✓) | Needs Improvement = circle the item |
|---|---|---|

- Write comments that will help the speaker, following this acronym:
    **S**pecific (For example, not "Good job" but "Excellent attention getter!")
    **H**elpful (Give ideas in a helpful way. Use "I" statements—"I'd like to see a visual aid.")
    **I**deas (Write down 3-4 ideas for improvement for this speech)
    **P**raise (Write down 3-4 things the speaker did well in this speech)

*Introduction*
__Grabbed attention __Revealed topic __Motivated audience __Established credibility
__Previewed main points

*Body*
            __Clear main points __Used clear transitions __Organization easy to follow
__Used sufficient supporting material __Variety of sources __Cited all supporting material
__Interesting, informative (not persuasive) topic __Adapted to audience
__Used audience analysis

*Presentational Slides*
__Easy to read __Impactful __ text minimal, __simple theme, __powerful images,
    __large fonts, __looked at computer display NOT the screen

*Delivery*
__Eye contact __Vocal variety __Used appropriate gestures __Used effective pauses
__Avoided vocal fillers (uh, uhms) __Used appropriate rate __Used creative language
__Used appropriate language __Avoided distractions

*Conclusion*
__Signaled ending __Summarized main points __Motivated audience
__Memorable ending or dramatic appeal

*Overall Speech Rating*
Choose one: ___Excellent ___Very Good ___Good ___Average ___Needs Improvement

What about this speech did you appreciate?

What suggestions for improvement would you give?

# Chapter 8 – Peer Feedback Forms

# Public Speaking Student Workbook
*Peer Feedback Form – Persuasive Speech #1 (Motivated Sequence)*

Speaker _____ Topic _____ Evaluator _____

*Instructions for this form:*
- Mark items using this system:

| Excellent = plus (+) | Average = check (✓) | Needs Improvement = circle the item |

- Write comments that will help the speaker, following this acronym:
    **S**pecific (For example, not "Good job" but "Excellent attention getter!")
    **H**elpful (Give ideas in a helpful way. Use "I" statements — "I'd like to see a visual aid.")
    **I**deas (Write down 3-4 ideas for improvement for this speech)
    **P**raise (Write down 3-4 things the speaker did well in this speech)

*Introduction*
__ATTENTION STEP __Grabbed attention __Revealed topic __Motivated audience
__Established credibility __Previewed main points

*Body*
__NEED STEP (clearly explained problem, related to audience needs)
__SATISFACTION STEP (clearly explained solution)
__VISUALIZATION STEP (presented strong benefits and/or consequences)
__Clear main points __Used sufficient supporting material __Cited all supporting material
__Interesting topic __Adapted to audience
__Used transitions __Used signal words

*Presentational Slides, if used*
__Easy to read __Impactful __ text minimal, __simple theme, __powerful images,
   __large fonts, __looked at computer display NOT the screen

*Delivery*
__Eye contact __Vocal variety __Used appropriate gestures __Used effective pauses
__Avoided vocal fillers (uh, uhms) __Used appropriate rate __Used creative language
__Used appropriate language __Avoided distractions

*Conclusion*
__ACTION STEP (boldly called audience to take specific action) __Signaled ending
__Summarized main points __Motivated audience __Memorable ending or dramatic appeal

*Overall Speech Rating*
Choose one: ___Excellent ___Very Good ___Good ___Average ___Needs Improvement
Was the speaker persuasive? Yes   No
What about this speech did you appreciate?

What do you suggest the speaker could do to be more persuasive or to improve this speech?

# Chapter 8 – Peer Feedback Forms

# Public Speaking Student Workbook
## *Peer Feedback Form — Persuasive Speech #1 (Motivated Sequence)*

Speaker _____ Topic _____ Evaluator _____

*Instructions for this form*:
- Mark items using this system:

| Excellent = plus (+) | Average = check (✓) | Needs Improvement = circle the item |

- Write comments that will help the speaker, following this acronym:
    **S**pecific (For example, not "Good job" but "Excellent attention getter!")
    **H**elpful (Give ideas in a helpful way. Use "I" statements — "I'd like to see a visual aid.")
    **I**deas (Write down 3-4 ideas for improvement for this speech)
    **P**raise (Write down 3-4 things the speaker did well in this speech)

*Introduction*
__ATTENTION STEP __Grabbed attention __Revealed topic __Motivated audience
__Established credibility __Previewed main points

*Body*
__NEED STEP (clearly explained problem, related to audience needs)
__SATISFACTION STEP (clearly explained solution)
__VISUALIZATION STEP (presented strong benefits and/or consequences)
__Clear main points __Used sufficient supporting material __Cited all supporting material
__Interesting topic __Adapted to audience
__Used transitions __Used signal words

*Presentational Slides, if used*
__Easy to read __impactful __ text minimal, __simple theme, __powerful images,
   __large fonts, __looked at computer display NOT the screen

*Delivery*
__Eye contact __Vocal variety __Used appropriate gestures __Used effective pauses
__Avoided vocal fillers (uh, uhms) __Used appropriate rate __Used creative language
__Used appropriate language __Avoided distractions

*Conclusion*
__ACTION STEP (boldly called audience to take specific action) __Signaled ending
__Summarized main points __Motivated audience __Memorable ending or dramatic appeal

*Overall Speech Rating*
Choose one: ___Excellent ___Very Good ___Good ___Average ___Needs Improvement
Was the speaker persuasive? Yes   No
What about this speech did you appreciate?

What do you suggest the speaker could do to be more persuasive or to improve this speech?

# Chapter 8 – Peer Feedback Forms

# Public Speaking Student Workbook
*Peer Feedback Form — Persuasive Speech #1 (Motivated Sequence)*

Speaker _____ Topic _____ Evaluator _____

*Instructions for this form:*
- Mark items using this system:

| Excellent = plus (+) | Average = check (✓) | Needs Improvement = circle the item |

- Write comments that will help the speaker, following this acronym:
    **S**pecific (For example, not "Good job" but "Excellent attention getter!")
    **H**elpful (Give ideas in a helpful way. Use "I" statements — "I'd like to see a visual aid.")
    **I**deas (Write down 3-4 ideas for improvement for this speech)
    **P**raise (Write down 3-4 things the speaker did well in this speech)

*Introduction*
__ATTENTION STEP __Grabbed attention __Revealed topic __Motivated audience
__Established credibility __Previewed main points

*Body*
__NEED STEP (clearly explained problem, related to audience needs)
__SATISFACTION STEP (clearly explained solution)
__VISUALIZATION STEP (presented strong benefits and/or consequences)
__Clear main points __Used sufficient supporting material __Cited all supporting material
__Interesting topic __Adapted to audience
__Used transitions __Used signal words

*Presentational Slides, if used*
__Easy to read __Impactful __text minimal, __simple theme, __powerful images,
    __large fonts, __looked at computer display NOT the screen

*Delivery*
__Eye contact __Vocal variety __Used appropriate gestures __Used effective pauses
__Avoided vocal fillers (uh, uhms) __Used appropriate rate __Used creative language
__Used appropriate language __Avoided distractions

*Conclusion*
__ACTION STEP (boldly called audience to take specific action) __Signaled ending
__Summarized main points __Motivated audience __Memorable ending or dramatic appeal

*Overall Speech Rating*
Choose one: ___Excellent ___Very Good ___Good ___Average ___Needs Improvement
Was the speaker persuasive? Yes   No
What about this speech did you appreciate?

What do you suggest the speaker could do to be more persuasive or to improve this speech?

# Chapter 8 – Peer Feedback Forms

# Public Speaking Student Workbook
## *Peer Feedback Form — Persuasive Speech #1 (Motivated Sequence)*

Speaker _____ Topic _____ Evaluator _____

*Instructions for this form*:
- Mark items using this system:

| Excellent = plus (+) | Average = check (✓) | Needs Improvement = circle the item |

- Write comments that will help the speaker, following this acronym:
    **S**pecific (For example, not "Good job" but "Excellent attention getter!")
    **H**elpful (Give ideas in a helpful way. Use "I" statements — "I'd like to see a visual aid.")
    **I**deas (Write down 3-4 ideas for improvement for this speech)
    **P**raise (Write down 3-4 things the speaker did well in this speech)

*Introduction*
__ATTENTION STEP __Grabbed attention __Revealed topic __Motivated audience
__Established credibility __Previewed main points

*Body*
__NEED STEP (clearly explained problem, related to audience needs)
__SATISFACTION STEP (clearly explained solution)
__VISUALIZATION STEP (presented strong benefits and/or consequences)
__Clear main points __Used sufficient supporting material __Cited all supporting material
__Interesting topic __Adapted to audience
__Used transitions __Used signal words

*Presentational Slides, if used*
__Easy to read __Impactful __ text minimal, __simple theme, __powerful images,
   __large fonts, __looked at computer display NOT the screen

*Delivery*
__Eye contact __Vocal variety __Used appropriate gestures __Used effective pauses
__Avoided vocal fillers (uh, uhms) __Used appropriate rate __Used creative language
__Used appropriate language __Avoided distractions

*Conclusion*
__ACTION STEP (boldly called audience to take specific action) __Signaled ending
__Summarized main points __Motivated audience __Memorable ending or dramatic appeal

*Overall Speech Rating*
Choose one: ___Excellent ___Very Good ___Good ___Average ___Needs Improvement
Was the speaker persuasive? Yes   No
What about this speech did you appreciate?

What do you suggest the speaker could do to be more persuasive or to improve this speech?

# Chapter 8 – Peer Feedback Forms

# Public Speaking Student Workbook
## *Peer Feedback Form — Persuasive Speech #1 (Motivated Sequence)*

Speaker _____ Topic _____ Evaluator _____

*Instructions for this form:*
- Mark items using this system:

| Excellent = plus (+) | Average = check (✓) | Needs Improvement = circle the item |
|---|---|---|

- Write comments that will help the speaker, following this acronym:
    **S**pecific (For example, not "Good job" but "Excellent attention getter!")
    **H**elpful (Give ideas in a helpful way. Use "I" statements — "I'd like to see a visual aid.")
    **I**deas (Write down 3-4 ideas for improvement for this speech)
    **P**raise (Write down 3-4 things the speaker did well in this speech)

*Introduction*
__ATTENTION STEP __Grabbed attention __Revealed topic __Motivated audience
__Established credibility __Previewed main points

*Body*
__NEED STEP (clearly explained problem, related to audience needs)
__SATISFACTION STEP (clearly explained solution)
__VISUALIZATION STEP (presented strong benefits and/or consequences)
__Clear main points __Used sufficient supporting material __Cited all supporting material
__Interesting topic __Adapted to audience
__Used transitions __Used signal words

*Presentational Slides, if used*
__Easy to read __Impactful __ text minimal, __simple theme, __powerful images,
   __large fonts, __looked at computer display NOT the screen

*Delivery*
__Eye contact __Vocal variety __Used appropriate gestures __Used effective pauses
__Avoided vocal fillers (uh, uhms) __Used appropriate rate __Used creative language
__Used appropriate language __Avoided distractions

*Conclusion*
__ACTION STEP (boldly called audience to take specific action) __Signaled ending
__Summarized main points __Motivated audience __Memorable ending or dramatic appeal

*Overall Speech Rating*
Choose one: ___Excellent ___Very Good ___Good ___Average ___Needs Improvement
Was the speaker persuasive? Yes   No
What about this speech did you appreciate?

What do you suggest the speaker could do to be more persuasive or to improve this speech?

# Chapter 8 – Peer Feedback Forms

# Public Speaking Student Workbook
*Peer Feedback Form—Persuasive Speech #1 (Motivated Sequence)*

Speaker _____ Topic _____ Evaluator _____

*Instructions for this form:*
- Mark items using this system:

  | Excellent = plus (+) | Average = check (✓) | Needs Improvement = circle the item |
  |---|---|---|

- Write comments that will help the speaker, following this acronym:
  **S**pecific (For example, not "Good job" but "Excellent attention getter!")
  **H**elpful (Give ideas in a helpful way. Use "I" statements—"I'd like to see a visual aid.")
  **I**deas (Write down 3-4 ideas for improvement for this speech)
  **P**raise (Write down 3-4 things the speaker did well in this speech)

*Introduction*
__ATTENTION STEP __Grabbed attention __Revealed topic __Motivated audience
__Established credibility __Previewed main points

*Body*
__NEED STEP (clearly explained problem, related to audience needs)
__SATISFACTION STEP (clearly explained solution)
__VISUALIZATION STEP (presented strong benefits and/or consequences)
__Clear main points __Used sufficient supporting material __Cited all supporting material
__Interesting topic __Adapted to audience
__Used transitions __Used signal words

*Presentational Slides, if used*
__Easy to read __Impactful __ text minimal, __simple theme, __powerful images,
  __large fonts, __looked at computer display NOT the screen

*Delivery*
__Eye contact __Vocal variety __Used appropriate gestures __Used effective pauses
__Avoided vocal fillers (uh, uhms) __Used appropriate rate __Used creative language
__Used appropriate language __Avoided distractions

*Conclusion*
__ACTION STEP (boldly called audience to take specific action) __Signaled ending
__Summarized main points __Motivated audience __Memorable ending or dramatic appeal

*Overall Speech Rating*
Choose one: ___Excellent ___Very Good ___Good ___Average ___Needs Improvement
Was the speaker persuasive? Yes   No
What about this speech did you appreciate?

What do you suggest the speaker could do to be more persuasive or to improve this speech?

# Chapter 8 – Peer Feedback Forms

# Public Speaking Student Workbook
## *Peer Feedback Form — Persuasive Speech #1 (Motivated Sequence)*

Speaker _____ Topic _____ Evaluator _____

*Instructions for this form:*
- Mark items using this system:

  | Excellent = plus (+) | Average = check (✓) | Needs Improvement = circle the item |
  |---|---|---|

- Write comments that will help the speaker, following this acronym:
  **S**pecific (For example, not "Good job" but "Excellent attention getter!")
  **H**elpful (Give ideas in a helpful way. Use "I" statements — "I'd like to see a visual aid.")
  **I**deas (Write down 3-4 ideas for improvement for this speech)
  **P**raise (Write down 3-4 things the speaker did well in this speech)

*Introduction*
__ATTENTION STEP __Grabbed attention __Revealed topic __Motivated audience
__Established credibility __Previewed main points

*Body*
__NEED STEP (clearly explained problem, related to audience needs)
__SATISFACTION STEP (clearly explained solution)
__VISUALIZATION STEP (presented strong benefits and/or consequences)
__Clear main points __Used sufficient supporting material __Cited all supporting material
__Interesting topic __Adapted to audience
__Used transitions __Used signal words

*Presentational Slides, if used*
__Easy to read __Impactful __ text minimal, __simple theme, __powerful images,
  __large fonts, __looked at computer display NOT the screen

*Delivery*
__Eye contact __Vocal variety __Used appropriate gestures __Used effective pauses
__Avoided vocal fillers (uh, uhms) __Used appropriate rate __Used creative language
__Used appropriate language __Avoided distractions

*Conclusion*
__ACTION STEP (boldly called audience to take specific action) __Signaled ending
__Summarized main points __Motivated audience __Memorable ending or dramatic appeal

*Overall Speech Rating*
Choose one: ___Excellent ___Very Good ___Good ___Average ___Needs Improvement
Was the speaker persuasive? Yes   No
What about this speech did you appreciate?

What do you suggest the speaker could do to be more persuasive or to improve this speech?

# Chapter 8 – Peer Feedback Forms

# Public Speaking Student Workbook
## Peer Feedback Form—Persuasive Speech #1 (Motivated Sequence)

Speaker _____ Topic _____ Evaluator _____

*Instructions for this form*:
- Mark items using this system:

  | Excellent = plus (+) | Average = check (✓) | Needs Improvement = circle the item |

- Write comments that will help the speaker, following this acronym:
    **S**pecific (For example, not "Good job" but "Excellent attention getter!")
    **H**elpful (Give ideas in a helpful way. Use "I" statements—"I'd like to see a visual aid.")
    **I**deas (Write down 3-4 ideas for improvement for this speech)
    **P**raise (Write down 3-4 things the speaker did well in this speech)

*Introduction*
__ATTENTION STEP __Grabbed attention __Revealed topic __Motivated audience
__Established credibility __Previewed main points

*Body*
__NEED STEP (clearly explained problem, related to audience needs)
__SATISFACTION STEP (clearly explained solution)
__VISUALIZATION STEP (presented strong benefits and/or consequences)
__Clear main points __Used sufficient supporting material __Cited all supporting material
__Interesting topic __Adapted to audience
__Used transitions __Used signal words

*Presentational Slides, if used*
__Easy to read __impactful __ text minimal, __simple theme, __powerful images,
  __large fonts, __looked at computer display NOT the screen

*Delivery*
__Eye contact __Vocal variety __Used appropriate gestures __Used effective pauses
__Avoided vocal fillers (uh, uhms) __Used appropriate rate __Used creative language
__Used appropriate language __Avoided distractions

*Conclusion*
__ACTION STEP (boldly called audience to take specific action) __Signaled ending
__Summarized main points __Motivated audience __Memorable ending or dramatic appeal

*Overall Speech Rating*
Choose one: ___Excellent ___Very Good ___Good ___Average ___Needs Improvement
Was the speaker persuasive? Yes   No
What about this speech did you appreciate?

What do you suggest the speaker could do to be more persuasive or to improve this speech?

# Chapter 8 – Peer Feedback Forms

## Public Speaking Student Workbook
*Peer Feedback Form — Persuasive Speech #1 (Motivated Sequence)*

Speaker _____ Topic _____ Evaluator _____

*Instructions for this form*:
- Mark items using this system:

| Excellent = plus (+) | Average = check (✓) | Needs Improvement = circle the item |

- Write comments that will help the speaker, following this acronym:
    **S**pecific (For example, not "Good job" but "Excellent attention getter!")
    **H**elpful (Give ideas in a helpful way. Use "I" statements — "I'd like to see a visual aid.")
    **I**deas (Write down 3-4 ideas for improvement for this speech)
    **P**raise (Write down 3-4 things the speaker did well in this speech)

*Introduction*
__ATTENTION STEP __Grabbed attention __Revealed topic __Motivated audience
__Established credibility __Previewed main points

*Body*
__NEED STEP (clearly explained problem, related to audience needs)
__SATISFACTION STEP (clearly explained solution)
__VISUALIZATION STEP (presented strong benefits and/or consequences)
__Clear main points __Used sufficient supporting material __Cited all supporting material
__Interesting topic __Adapted to audience
__Used transitions __Used signal words

*Presentational Slides, if used*
__Easy to read __Impactful __ text minimal, __simple theme, __powerful images,
   __large fonts, __looked at computer display NOT the screen

*Delivery*
__Eye contact __Vocal variety __Used appropriate gestures __Used effective pauses
__Avoided vocal fillers (uh, uhms) __Used appropriate rate __Used creative language
__Used appropriate language __Avoided distractions

*Conclusion*
__ACTION STEP (boldly called audience to take specific action) __Signaled ending
__Summarized main points __Motivated audience __Memorable ending or dramatic appeal

*Overall Speech Rating*
Choose one: ___Excellent ___Very Good ___Good ___Average ___Needs Improvement
Was the speaker persuasive? Yes   No
What about this speech did you appreciate?

What do you suggest the speaker could do to be more persuasive or to improve this speech?

# Chapter 8 – Peer Feedback Forms

# Public Speaking Student Workbook
## *Peer Feedback Form — Persuasive Speech #2*

Speaker _____ Topic _____ Evaluator _____

*Instructions for this form*:
- Mark items using this system:

| Excellent = plus (+) | Average = check (✓) | Needs Improvement = circle the item |

- Write comments that will help the speaker, following this acronym:
    **S**pecific (For example, not "Good job" but "Excellent attention getter!")
    **H**elpful (Give ideas in a helpful way. Use "I" statements — "I'd like to see a visual aid.")
    **I**deas (Write down 3-4 ideas for improvement for this speech)
    **P**raise (Write down 3-4 things the speaker did well in this speech)

*Introduction*
__Grabbed attention __Revealed topic __Motivated audience __Established credibility
__Previewed main points

*Body*
__Clear main points __Used sufficient supporting material __Cited all supporting material
    __Used credible, reliable sources __Logical reasoning __Used emotional examples &
    appeals
__Used audience analysis __Adapted to audience
__Used transitions __Chose an Interesting topic __Stayed persuasive, not informative


*Presentational Slides*
__Easy to read __Impactful __ text minimal, __simple theme, __powerful images,
    __large fonts, __looked at computer display NOT the screen

*Delivery*
__Eye contact __Vocal variety __Used appropriate gestures __Used effective pauses
__Avoided vocal fillers (uh, uhms) __Used appropriate rate __Used creative language
__Used appropriate language __Avoided distractions


*Conclusion*
__Signaled ending __Summarized main points __Motivated audience
__Memorable ending or dramatic appeal

*Overall Speech Rating*
Choose one: ___Excellent ___Very Good ___Good ___Average ___Needs Improvement

Was the speaker persuasive? Yes   No
What about this speech did you appreciate?

What do you suggest the speaker could do to be more persuasive or to improve this speech?

__# Chapter 8 – Peer Feedback Forms__

# Public Speaking Student Workbook
## Peer Feedback Form – Persuasive Speech #2

Speaker _____ Topic _____ Evaluator _____

*Instructions for this form*:
- Mark items using this system:

| Excellent = plus (+) | Average = check (✓) | Needs Improvement = circle the item |
|---|---|---|

- Write comments that will help the speaker, following this acronym:
    **S**pecific (For example, not "Good job" but "Excellent attention getter!")
    **H**elpful (Give ideas in a helpful way. Use "I" statements – "I'd like to see a visual aid.")
    **I**deas (Write down 3-4 ideas for improvement for this speech)
    **P**raise (Write down 3-4 things the speaker did well in this speech)

*Introduction*
__Grabbed attention __Revealed topic __Motivated audience __Established credibility
__Previewed main points

*Body*
__Clear main points __Used sufficient supporting material __Cited all supporting material
    __Used credible, reliable sources __Logical reasoning __Used emotional examples & appeals __Used audience analysis __Adapted to audience
__Used transitions __Chose an Interesting topic __Stayed persuasive, not informative

*Presentational Slides*
__Easy to read __Impactful __ text minimal, __simple theme, __powerful images,
    __large fonts, __looked at computer display NOT the screen

*Delivery*
__Eye contact __Vocal variety __Used appropriate gestures __Used effective pauses
__Avoided vocal fillers (uh, uhms) __Used appropriate rate __Used creative language
__Used appropriate language __Avoided distractions

*Conclusion*
__Signaled ending __Summarized main points __Motivated audience
__Memorable ending or dramatic appeal

*Overall Speech Rating*
Choose one: __Excellent __Very Good __Good __Average __Needs Improvement

Was the speaker persuasive? Yes   No
What about this speech did you appreciate?

What do you suggest the speaker could do to be more persuasive or to improve this speech?

# Chapter 8 – Peer Feedback Forms

# Public Speaking Student Workbook
## Peer Feedback Form — Persuasive Speech #2

Speaker _____ Topic _____ Evaluator _____

*Instructions for this form*:
- Mark items using this system:

| Excellent = plus (+) | Average = check (✓) | Needs Improvement = circle the item |
|---|---|---|

- Write comments that will help the speaker, following this acronym:
    **S**pecific (For example, not "Good job" but "Excellent attention getter!")
    **H**elpful (Give ideas in a helpful way. Use "I" statements — "I'd like to see a visual aid.")
    **I**deas (Write down 3-4 ideas for improvement for this speech)
    **P**raise (Write down 3-4 things the speaker did well in this speech)

*Introduction*
__Grabbed attention __Revealed topic __Motivated audience __Established credibility
__Previewed main points

*Body*
__Clear main points __Used sufficient supporting material __Cited all supporting material
__Used credible, reliable sources __Logical reasoning __Used emotional examples & appeals
__Used audience analysis __Adapted to audience
__Used transitions __Chose an Interesting topic __Stayed persuasive, not informative

*Presentational Slides*
__Easy to read __Impactful __ text minimal, __simple theme, __powerful images,
   __large fonts, __looked at computer display NOT the screen

*Delivery*
__Eye contact __Vocal variety __Used appropriate gestures __Used effective pauses
__Avoided vocal fillers (uh, uhms) __Used appropriate rate __Used creative language
__Used appropriate language __Avoided distractions

*Conclusion*
__Signaled ending __Summarized main points __Motivated audience
__Memorable ending or dramatic appeal

*Overall Speech Rating*
Choose one: ___Excellent ___Very Good ___Good ___Average ___Needs Improvement

Was the speaker persuasive? Yes   No
What about this speech did you appreciate?

What do you suggest the speaker could do to be more persuasive or to improve this speech?

# Chapter 8 – Peer Feedback Forms

# Public Speaking Student Workbook
## Peer Feedback Form — Persuasive Speech #2

Speaker _____ Topic _____ Evaluator _____

*Instructions for this form*:
- Mark items using this system:

| Excellent = plus (+) | Average = check (✓) | Needs Improvement = circle the item |
|---|---|---|

- Write comments that will help the speaker, following this acronym:
    **S**pecific (For example, not "Good job" but "Excellent attention getter!")
    **H**elpful (Give ideas in a helpful way. Use "I" statements — "I'd like to see a visual aid.")
    **I**deas (Write down 3-4 ideas for improvement for this speech)
    **P**raise (Write down 3-4 things the speaker did well in this speech)

*Introduction*
__Grabbed attention __Revealed topic __Motivated audience __Established credibility
__Previewed main points

*Body*
__Clear main points __Used sufficient supporting material __Cited all supporting material
__Used credible, reliable sources __Logical reasoning __Used emotional examples & appeals
__Used audience analysis __Adapted to audience
__Used transitions __Chose an Interesting topic __Stayed persuasive, not informative

*Presentational Slides*
__Easy to read __Impactful __ text minimal, __simple theme, __powerful images,
    __large fonts, __looked at computer display NOT the screen

*Delivery*
__Eye contact __Vocal variety __Used appropriate gestures __Used effective pauses
__Avoided vocal fillers (uh, uhms) __Used appropriate rate __Used creative language
__Used appropriate language __Avoided distractions

*Conclusion*
__Signaled ending __Summarized main points __Motivated audience
__Memorable ending or dramatic appeal

*Overall Speech Rating*
Choose one: ___Excellent ___Very Good ___Good ___Average ___Needs Improvement

Was the speaker persuasive? Yes   No
What about this speech did you appreciate?

What do you suggest the speaker could do to be more persuasive or to improve this speech?

# Chapter 8 – Peer Feedback Forms

# Public Speaking Student Workbook
## Peer Feedback Form — Persuasive Speech #2

Speaker _____ Topic _____ Evaluator _____

*Instructions for this form:*
- Mark items using this system:

  | Excellent = plus (+) | Average = check (✓) | Needs Improvement = circle the item |

- Write comments that will help the speaker, following this acronym:
    **S**pecific (For example, not "Good job" but "Excellent attention getter!")
    **H**elpful (Give ideas in a helpful way. Use "I" statements — "I'd like to see a visual aid.")
    **I**deas (Write down 3-4 ideas for improvement for this speech)
    **P**raise (Write down 3-4 things the speaker did well in this speech)

*Introduction*
__Grabbed attention __Revealed topic __Motivated audience __Established credibility
__Previewed main points

*Body*
__Clear main points __Used sufficient supporting material __Cited all supporting material
__Used credible, reliable sources __Logical reasoning __Used emotional examples & appeals
__Used audience analysis __Adapted to audience
__Used transitions __Chose an Interesting topic __Stayed persuasive, not informative

*Presentational Slides*
__Easy to read __Impactful __ text minimal, __simple theme, __powerful images,
   __large fonts, __looked at computer display NOT the screen

*Delivery*
__Eye contact __Vocal variety __Used appropriate gestures __Used effective pauses
__Avoided vocal fillers (uh, uhms) __Used appropriate rate __Used creative language
__Used appropriate language __Avoided distractions

*Conclusion*
__Signaled ending __Summarized main points __Motivated audience
__Memorable ending or dramatic appeal

*Overall Speech Rating*
Choose one: __Excellent __Very Good __Good __Average __Needs Improvement

Was the speaker persuasive? Yes   No
What about this speech did you appreciate?

   What do you suggest the speaker could do to be more persuasive or to improve this speech?

# Chapter 8 – Peer Feedback Forms

# Public Speaking Student Workbook
## Peer Feedback Form — Persuasive Speech #2

Speaker _____ Topic _____ Evaluator _____

*Instructions for this form*:
- Mark items using this system:

| Excellent = plus (+) | Average = check (✓) | Needs Improvement = circle the item |

- Write comments that will help the speaker, following this acronym:
  **S**pecific (For example, not "Good job" but "Excellent attention getter!")
  **H**elpful (Give ideas in a helpful way. Use "I" statements — "I'd like to see a visual aid.")
  **I**deas (Write down 3-4 ideas for improvement for this speech)
  **P**raise (Write down 3-4 things the speaker did well in this speech)

*Introduction*
__Grabbed attention __Revealed topic __Motivated audience __Established credibility
__Previewed main points

*Body*
__Clear main points __Used sufficient supporting material __Cited all supporting material
__Used credible, reliable sources __Logical reasoning __Used emotional examples & appeals
__Used audience analysis __Adapted to audience
__Used transitions __Chose an Interesting topic __Stayed persuasive, not informative

*Presentational Slides*
__Easy to read __Impactful __ text minimal, __simple theme, __powerful images,
  __large fonts, __looked at computer display NOT the screen

*Delivery*
__Eye contact __Vocal variety __Used appropriate gestures __Used effective pauses
__Avoided vocal fillers (uh, uhms) __Used appropriate rate __Used creative language
__Used appropriate language __Avoided distractions

*Conclusion*
__Signaled ending __Summarized main points __Motivated audience
__Memorable ending or dramatic appeal

*Overall Speech Rating*
Choose one: ___Excellent ___Very Good ___Good ___Average ___Needs Improvement

Was the speaker persuasive? Yes   No
What about this speech did you appreciate?

What do you suggest the speaker could do to be more persuasive or to improve this speech?

# Chapter 8 – Peer Feedback Forms

# Public Speaking Student Workbook
## Peer Feedback Form — Persuasive Speech #2

Speaker _____ Topic _____ Evaluator _____

*Instructions for this form:*
- Mark items using this system:

| Excellent = plus (+) | Average = check (✓) | Needs Improvement = circle the item |

- Write comments that will help the speaker, following this acronym:
    **S**pecific (For example, not "Good job" but "Excellent attention getter!")
    **H**elpful (Give ideas in a helpful way. Use "I" statements — "I'd like to see a visual aid.")
    **I**deas (Write down 3-4 ideas for improvement for this speech)
    **P**raise (Write down 3-4 things the speaker did well in this speech)

*Introduction*
__Grabbed attention __Revealed topic __Motivated audience __Established credibility
__Previewed main points

*Body*
__Clear main points __Used sufficient supporting material __Cited all supporting material
__Used credible, reliable sources __Logical reasoning __Used emotional examples & appeals
__Used audience analysis __Adapted to audience
__Used transitions __Chose an Interesting topic __Stayed persuasive, not informative

*Presentational Slides*
__Easy to read __Impactful __ text minimal, __simple theme, __powerful images,
    __large fonts, __looked at computer display NOT the screen

*Delivery*
__Eye contact __Vocal variety __Used appropriate gestures __Used effective pauses
__Avoided vocal fillers (uh, uhms) __Used appropriate rate __Used creative language
__Used appropriate language __Avoided distractions

*Conclusion*
__Signaled ending __Summarized main points __Motivated audience
__Memorable ending or dramatic appeal

*Overall Speech Rating*
Choose one: ___Excellent ___Very Good ___Good ___Average ___Needs Improvement

Was the speaker persuasive? Yes   No
What about this speech did you appreciate?

What do you suggest the speaker could do to be more persuasive or to improve this speech?

# Chapter 8 – Peer Feedback Forms

# Public Speaking Student Workbook
## Peer Feedback Form — Persuasive Speech #2

Speaker _____ Topic _____ Evaluator _____

*Instructions for this form:*
- Mark items using this system:

| Excellent = plus (+) | Average = check (✓) | Needs Improvement = circle the item |
|---|---|---|

- Write comments that will help the speaker, following this acronym:
    **S**pecific (For example, not "Good job" but "Excellent attention getter!")
    **H**elpful (Give ideas in a helpful way. Use "I" statements — "I'd like to see a visual aid.")
    **I**deas (Write down 3-4 ideas for improvement for this speech)
    **P**raise (Write down 3-4 things the speaker did well in this speech)

*Introduction*
__Grabbed attention __Revealed topic __Motivated audience __Established credibility
__Previewed main points

*Body*
__Clear main points __Used sufficient supporting material __Cited all supporting material
__Used credible, reliable sources __Logical reasoning __Used emotional examples & appeals
__Used audience analysis __Adapted to audience
__Used transitions __Chose an Interesting topic __Stayed persuasive, not informative

*Presentational Slides*
__Easy to read __Impactful __ text minimal, __simple theme, __powerful images,
   __large fonts, __looked at computer display NOT the screen

*Delivery*
__Eye contact __Vocal variety __Used appropriate gestures __Used effective pauses
__Avoided vocal fillers (uh, uhms) __Used appropriate rate __Used creative language
__Used appropriate language __Avoided distractions

*Conclusion*
__Signaled ending __Summarized main points __Motivated audience
__Memorable ending or dramatic appeal

*Overall Speech Rating*
Choose one: ___Excellent ___Very Good ___Good ___Average ___Needs Improvement

Was the speaker persuasive? Yes   No
What about this speech did you appreciate?

What do you suggest the speaker could do to be more persuasive or to improve this speech?

# Chapter 8 – Peer Feedback Forms

# Public Speaking Student Workbook
## Peer Feedback Form — Persuasive Speech #2

Speaker _____ Topic _____ Evaluator _____

*Instructions for this form:*
- Mark items using this system:

| Excellent = plus (+) | Average = check (✓) | Needs Improvement = circle the item |

- Write comments that will help the speaker, following this acronym:
    **S**pecific (For example, not "Good job" but "Excellent attention getter!")
    **H**elpful (Give ideas in a helpful way. Use "I" statements — "I'd like to see a visual aid.")
    **I**deas (Write down 3-4 ideas for improvement for this speech)
    **P**raise (Write down 3-4 things the speaker did well in this speech)

*Introduction*
__Grabbed attention __Revealed topic __Motivated audience __Established credibility
__Previewed main points

*Body*
__Clear main points __Used sufficient supporting material __Cited all supporting material
__Used credible, reliable sources __Logical reasoning __Used emotional examples & appeals
__Used audience analysis __Adapted to audience
__Used transitions __Chose an Interesting topic __Stayed persuasive, not informative

*Presentational Slides*
__Easy to read __Impactful __ text minimal, __simple theme, __powerful images,
   __large fonts, __looked at computer display NOT the screen

*Delivery*
__Eye contact __Vocal variety __Used appropriate gestures __Used effective pauses
__Avoided vocal fillers (uh, uhms) __Used appropriate rate __Used creative language
__Used appropriate language __Avoided distractions

*Conclusion*
__Signaled ending __Summarized main points __Motivated audience
__Memorable ending or dramatic appeal

*Overall Speech Rating*
Choose one: ___Excellent ___Very Good ___Good ___Average ___Needs Improvement

Was the speaker persuasive? Yes   No
What about this speech did you appreciate?

What do you suggest the speaker could do to be more persuasive or to improve this speech?

# Extra Credit

# 9

## EXTRA CREDIT

CONSULTING FORM

SPEECH EVALUATION TEMPLATE

# Extra Credit

Public Speaking Student Workbook
*EXTRA-CREDIT SPEECH CENTER CONSULTING FORM*

NAME: _____ CLASS TIME: _____

## OBJECTIVES

1. To get extra help to improve your next speech grade.

2. To work with a speech instructor/consultant on researching your speech topic, gathering supporting material, writing your outline, or delivering your speech and watching it before you give it in class.

## INSTRUCTIONS:
You will need to drop by the Speech Center and ask the instructor/consultant to help you with your next speech. Ask for help you with any aspect of developing your next speech (e.g., researching the topic, gathering supporting material, organization and outlining, or delivering your speech and watching it, etc.). Then complete this form.

## SUMMARY:
Please summarize below (and on the back of this page) in detail how the consulting helped you and then ask the consultant to sign and stamp this form.

## EVALUATION CRITERIA
You can receive up to 10 Extra-credit Points for receiving consultation in the speech center and summarizing how the help assisted you in preparing for your next speech.

## DATE AND TIME

## LAB INSTRUCTOR'S STAMP

# Extra Credit

Public Speaking Student Workbook

## *EXTRA-CREDIT SPEECH EVALUATION*

NAME: _____ CLASS TIME: _____

### OBJECTIVES

1. To observe a skilled speaker for the purpose of learning more about effective communication techniques.

2. To critique, analyze, and evaluate an outside speaker based on the important speech making concepts studied in this class.

### INSTRUCTIONS

Observe a professional speaker. <u>You must be an audience member</u> who listens to a person give a speech (e.g., a political speaker/candidate, a campus speaker, a guest speaker for an organization, a church speaker/ minister/ rabbi/ priest, or etc.) The speaker cannot be a professor/instructor in one your classes. Critique the speaker and speech by using the following evaluation form.

### EVALUATION CRITERIA

You can receive up to 10 Points (extra-credit) for critically evaluating the speaker and speech based on the important criteria for effective speech making that we have studied in this class.

# Extra Credit

Public Speaking Student Workbook

## *EXTRA-CREDIT SPEAKER EVALUATION FORM*

**NAME** _____ **DATE:** _____

**SPEAKER** _____

**SUBJECT** _____

**AUDIENCE** _____

**OCCASION/EVENT** _____

1. Was there an introducer for the speaker? If so, did the introducer give information about the speaker and create a welcoming environment? Explain.

2. What was the main speaker's purpose (to inform, to persuade, to entertain)?

3. What was the speaker's central idea as you understood it?

4. What was the speaker's knowledge of the topic (credibility)?

5. Who was the target audience?

6. What did the speaker do to adapt to the audience and the occasion?

7. Did the speaker get the audience's attention and interest? How?

8. What organizational pattern did the speaker use for his/her main points?

# Extra Credit

9. What were the most notable strengths and weaknesses of the organization or content?

10. Did the speaker use any stylistic language techniques (e.g., similes, metaphors, repetition, parallelism, alliteration, antithesis, etc.)?

11. Was the use of language effective? Explain.

12. What were the most effective aspects of the speaker's delivery (i.e. volume, conversational style, rate, pauses, vocal variety, pronunciation, articulation, personal appearance, body movements, gestures, eye contact)?

13. Did the speaker use Presentational Slides or visual aids? Were they used effectively?

14. What "Areas for Improvement" do you suggest for the speaker's delivery?

15. What evidence did the speaker offer to support his/her points?

16. What emotional or motivational appeals did the speaker use?

17. Overall, how would you evaluate the effectiveness of the speech?

18. From this speaker, what did you learn to help you improve your speeches?

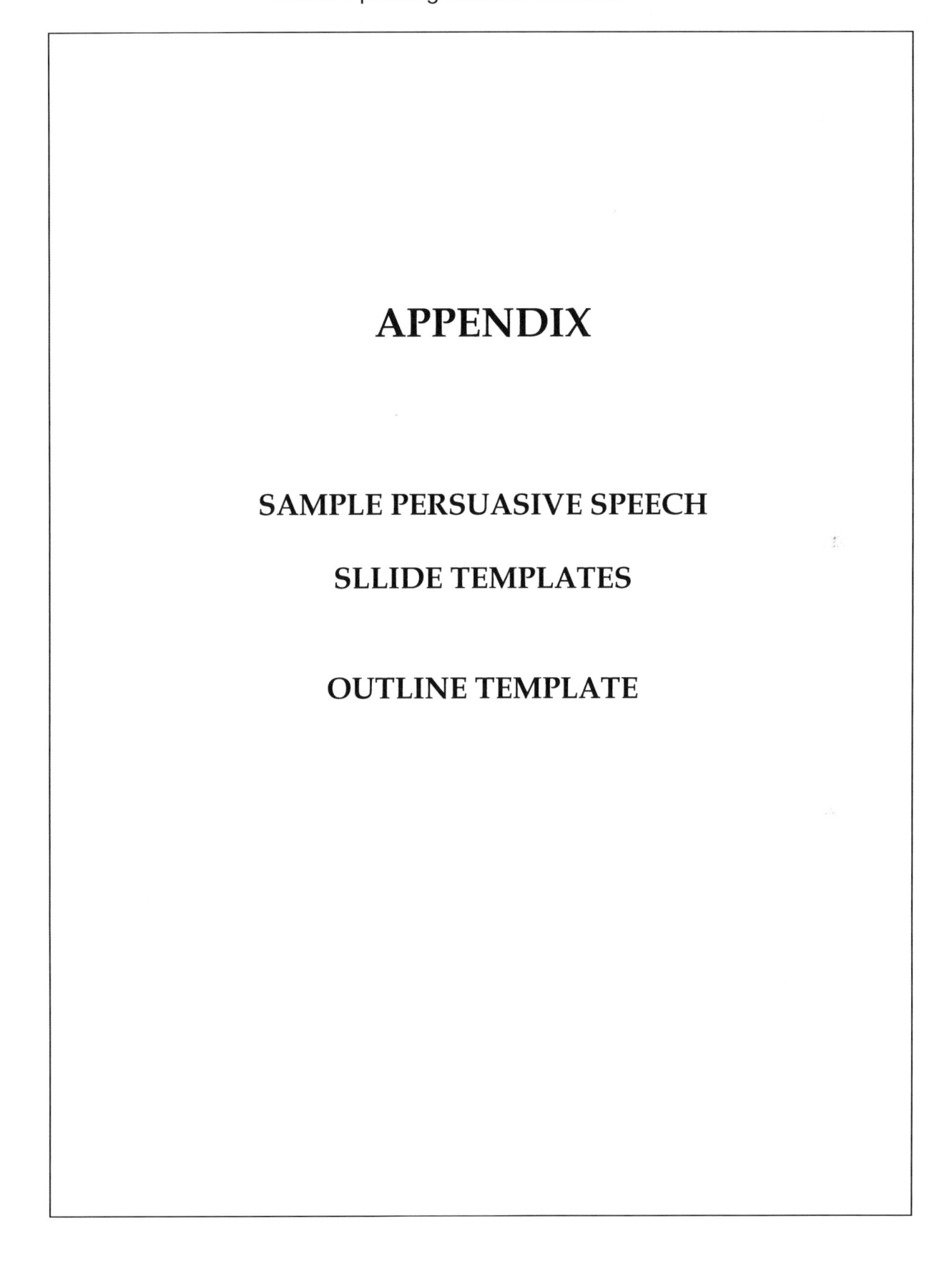

# APPENDIX

## SAMPLE PERSUASIVE SPEECH

## SLLIDE TEMPLATES

## OUTLINE TEMPLATE

# Appendix

Public Speaking Student Workbook
*SAMPLE PERSUASIVE SPEECH #2 OUTLINE*
*TANNING BEDS ARE BAD FOR YOUR HEALTH\**

Organization Pattern: Problem-Solution/ Monroe's Motivated Sequence
General Purpose: To persuade
Specific Purpose: To persuade my audience to stop using tanning beds for three reasons.
Central Idea: You should stop using tanning beds because it's extremely bad for your health, alternatives give you almost equal results, and if you don't, it can negatively impact your future.

Introduction:
Attention: Did you know that using a tanning bed before the age of 35 increases your risk of getting melanoma (the deadliest form of skin cancer) by 75 percent? This statistic is from the World Health Organizations *International Agency for Research on Cancer* on the FDA U.S. Food & Drug Administration's website, April 12, 2012. Tanning has become a very popular activity for everyone living in the United States. In fact, on an average day, more than a million people go to tanning salons.
Importance: It is important to know the risks of tanning beds and how they can affect your future, so you can take appropriate actions now to avoid deadly cancers.
Creditability: I have both stopped tanning a year ago and began studying it.
Preview: Today, I *will discuss a common activity that is bad for your health, some possible alternatives with almost equal results, and how if don't stop now, tanning can negatively impact your future.

Body:
I. (**Problem/Need**): According to a *Lancet Journal* article by Dr. Maria Chung published on July 29, 2009 and cited on MSNBC: "International cancer experts have moved tanning beds and other sources of ultraviolet radiation into the top cancer risk category, deeming them as deadly as arsenic and mustard gas."
   A. Tanning beds can cause skin cancer and eye problems.
     1. UVA and UVB rays cause skin cancer, and although many tanning salons claim that their beds are "safe", they aren't. Tanning beds go past limit of UV rays safe exposure.
     2. Tanning beds also affect the eyes. While tanning, you are putting your eyes at an increased risk of developing burns and cataracts, which is a clouding of the eye's natural lens. Cataracts can cause vision loss and is the top cause of blindness in the world today.
   B. Tanning beds are worse than the actual sun.
     1. Tanning beds are not yet considered to be a medical device and so they are not regulated by health agencies.
     2. According to an Astro nutrition article from stronutriiont.com, entitled *Tanning Beds Worse than the Sun*, published on April 13, 2010: "While the FDA for instance does regulate the amount of UV emissions from the lamps used in the beds, as of yet the beds do not need FDA approval."

(**Transition:** Now that I have talked about the health effects tanning can have, I will discuss an alternative to tanning beds.)

II. (**Solution/Satisfaction**): When there are such great alternatives to tanning beds, there is no need to use them anymore.
   A. Spray tans and self-tanners now look like a natural tan, but without all of the added consequences
     1. No longer are the days of orange-looking self-tanners; they look natural now.
       a. Examples of self-tanners are Fake Bake, Jergens Natural Glow, and Olay Sun.
       b. The two main types of spray tanning are airbrush and the Mystic Tan machine.
     2. You won't be putting your valuable health in danger with these options.

## Appendix

  B. These alternatives are affordable and make you look tanner much faster than beds.
    1. Super expensive tanning lotions and rising membership costs to tanning salons will no longer be an issue for your budget.
    2. You may have to spend weeks or months in tanning beds to achieve the level of tan you want. With spray tans and self-tanners, you can look just as tan in only a matter of hours.
  C. Surprisingly, even tanning outside in the sun is a slightly better alternative than using tanning beds, because according to Dr. David Zagota's article 'Tanning Beds vs. The Sun' from livestrong.com, published on May 5, 2011, "The sunlamps used in tanning salons emit UVA that is 12 times that of the sun, according to the Skin Cancer Foundation."

**(Transition: Now that I have discussed some alternatives, let's look at what can happen if you continue to use tanning beds.)**

III. **(Practicality/Visualization)** Tanning beds can negatively impact your future, even if you can't see it now.
  A. The most obvious future effects of tanning beds are wrinkles and leathery-looking skin so picture yourself with skin that is embarrassing or even worse is developing cancer lesions.
  B. According to Audrey Kunin, M.D., in Derma Doctor, entitled Tanning Bed Taboo: "The UVA rays of tanning beds can penetrate down into the dermis. These rays can cause damage to cellular DNA, collagen and elastin fibers, dermal blood vessels and other deeply situated structures". This is what causes us to get wrinkles and horrible leathery skin texture.
  C. Some people believe that skin cancers show up right away, so if they haven't had it yet, it means they can continue tanning "safely". But in reality, it can show up now or years in the future.
  D. Now picture yourself tanned and feeling confident from using a spray tan; it took only a few minutes and you are happy you will not face the side effects of wrinkled skin or cancer.

## Conclusion:
**Sign Post**: In conclusion, I have discussed the three reasons to stop using tanning beds.
**Summary**: Tanning is extremely bad for your health, alternatives give you almost equal results, and you can face a healthy future not a negative one.
**Call To Action**: Imagine yourself in 20 years sitting by the pool, and people keep negatively staring at you because your skin looks like leather with wrinkles or you have splotches from cancers that have been removed. This is not a pretty picture. If you don't want to face these situations, please STOP using tanning beds right now! Instead stop by a drug store and pick up an inexpensive can of spray tan.

## References:
AstroNutrition (2010). Tanning beds worse than the sun. Retrieved from **http://astronutrition.com/blog/tanning_beds_worse_sun** (2012, April 5). .
Cheng, M (2009). Tanning beds can be as deadly as arsenic: Study. *Associated Press*. Retrieved from http://www.msnbc.msn.com/id/32187497/ns/health-cancer/t/study-tanning-beds-can-be-deadly-arsenic/#.T2UStdVW2So (2012, April 6).
FDA U. S. Food & Drug Administration (2012). Indoor tanning: The risk of ultraviolet rays. Retrieved from http://www.fda.gov/forconsumers/consumerupdates/ucm186687.htm (2012, April 6).
Kunin, A. (2012). Tanning bed taboo. DermaDoctor (Online). Retrieved from **http://www.dermadoctor.com/article_Tanning-Bed-Taboo_175.html** (2012, April 6).
Zagata, D. (2011). Tanning beds vs. the sun. Livestrong. Retrieved from
    http://www.livestrong.com/article/68629-tanning-beds-vs.-sun (2012, April 4).

*This speech outline was adapted from one originally written by Emily Niewohner and Taylor Ira and used by permission of the speakers.

# Public Speaking Student Workbook
## *TEMPLATES FOR PRESENTATIONAL SLIDES*

**Attention Slide**
☐Photo ☐Illustration ☐Chart ☐Text

**Preview Slide**
☐Photo ☐Illustration ☐Chart ☐Text

**Main Point One Slide**
☐Photo ☐Illustration ☐Chart ☐Text

**Main Point Two Slide**
☐Photo ☐Illustration ☐Chart ☐Text

**Main Point Three Slide**
☐Photo ☐Illustration ☐Chart ☐Text

**Conclusion/Ending Slide**
☐Photo ☐Illustration ☐Chart ☐Text

# Appendix

# Public Speaking Student Workbook
## *TEMPLATES FOR PRESENTATIONAL SLIDES*

**Attention Slide**
☐Photo ☐Illustration ☐Chart ☐Text

**Preview Slide**
☐Photo ☐Illustration ☐Chart ☐Text

**Main Point One Slide**
☐Photo ☐Illustration ☐Chart ☐Text

**Main Point Two Slide**
☐Photo ☐Illustration ☐Chart ☐Text

**Main Point Three Slide**
☐Photo ☐Illustration ☐Chart ☐Text

**Conclusion/Ending Slide**
☐Photo ☐Illustration ☐Chart ☐Text

# Appendix

# Public Speaking Student Workbook
## *TEMPLATES FOR PRESENTATIONAL SLIDES*

**Attention Slide**
☐Photo ☐Illustration ☐Chart ☐Text

**Preview Slide**
☐Photo ☐Illustration ☐Chart ☐Text

**Main Point One Slide**
☐Photo ☐Illustration ☐Chart ☐Text

**Main Point Two Slide**
☐Photo ☐Illustration ☐Chart ☐Text

**Main Point Three Slide**
☐Photo ☐Illustration ☐Chart ☐Text

**Conclusion/Ending Slide**
☐Photo ☐Illustration ☐Chart ☐Text

# Appendix

# Public Speaking Student Workbook
## *TEMPLATES FOR PRESENTATIONAL SLIDES*

**Attention Slide**
☐Photo ☐Illustration ☐Chart ☐Text

**Preview Slide**
☐Photo ☐Illustration ☐Chart ☐Text

**Main Point One Slide**
☐Photo ☐Illustration ☐Chart ☐Text

**Main Point Two Slide**
☐Photo ☐Illustration ☐Chart ☐Text

**Main Point Three Slide**
☐Photo ☐Illustration ☐Chart ☐Text

**Conclusion/Ending Slide**
☐Photo ☐Illustration ☐Chart ☐Text

# Appendix

# Public Speaking Student Workbook
## *TEMPLATES FOR PRESENTATIONAL SLIDES*

**Attention Slide**
☐Photo ☐Illustration ☐Chart ☐Text

**Preview Slide**
☐Photo ☐Illustration ☐Chart ☐Text

**Main Point One Slide**
☐Photo ☐Illustration ☐Chart ☐Text

**Main Point Two Slide**
☐Photo ☐Illustration ☐Chart ☐Text

**Main Point Three Slide**
☐Photo ☐Illustration ☐Chart ☐Text

**Conclusion/Ending Slide**
☐Photo ☐Illustration ☐Chart ☐Text

# Appendix

# Public Speaking Student Workbook
## *TEMPLATES FOR PRESENTATIONAL SLIDES*

**Attention Slide**
☐Photo ☐Illustration ☐Chart ☐Text

**Preview Slide**
☐Photo ☐Illustration ☐Chart ☐Text

**Main Point One Slide**
☐Photo ☐Illustration ☐Chart ☐Text

**Main Point Two Slide**
☐Photo ☐Illustration ☐Chart ☐Text

**Main Point Three Slide**
☐Photo ☐Illustration ☐Chart ☐Text

**Conclusion/Ending Slide**
☐Photo ☐Illustration ☐Chart ☐Text

# Appendix

Public Speaking Student Workbook

**Presentation Outline** (fold in half)

Name:
Speech Title:
Introduction:
Attention Getter:
Importance:
Credibility:
Preview:
Body:
I. First,
   A.
      1. Supporting Material
      2.
   B.
      1.
      2.
   C.
      1.
      2.

**(Transition):** Now that
II. Second,
   A.
      1. Supporting Material
      2.
   B.
      1.
      2.

**(Transition):** After you have.
III. Third,
   A.
      1.
      2.
   B.
      1.
      2.

**In Conclusion,**
Recap Points

Importance to audience:

Memorable Ending:

# Appendix

# Public Speaking Student Workbook

## Presentation Outline (fold in half)

Name:
Speech Title:

Introduction:
Attention Getter:

Importance:

Credibility:

Preview:

Body:
I. First,
  A.
    1. Supporting Material
    2.
  B.
    1.
    2.
  C.
    1.
    2.

(**Transition**: Now that

II. Second,
  A.
    1. Supporting Material
    2.
  B.
    1.
    2.

(**Transition**: After you have.

III. Third,
  A.
    1.
    2.
  B.
    1.
    2.

**In Conclusion,**
Recap Points

Importance to audience:

Memorable Ending:

# Appendix

**Presentation Outline** (fold in half)

Name:
Speech Title:
Introduction:
Attention Getter:
Importance:
Credibility:
Preview:
Body:
I. First,
   A.
      1. Supporting Material
      2.
   B.
      1.
      2.
   C.
      1.
      2.

(**Transition**): Now that

II. Second,
   A.
      1. Supporting Material
      2.
   B.
      1.
      2.

(**Transition**): After you have.

III. Third,
   A.
      1.
      2.
   B.
      1.
      2.

**In Conclusion,**
Recap Points

Importance to audience:

Memorable Ending:

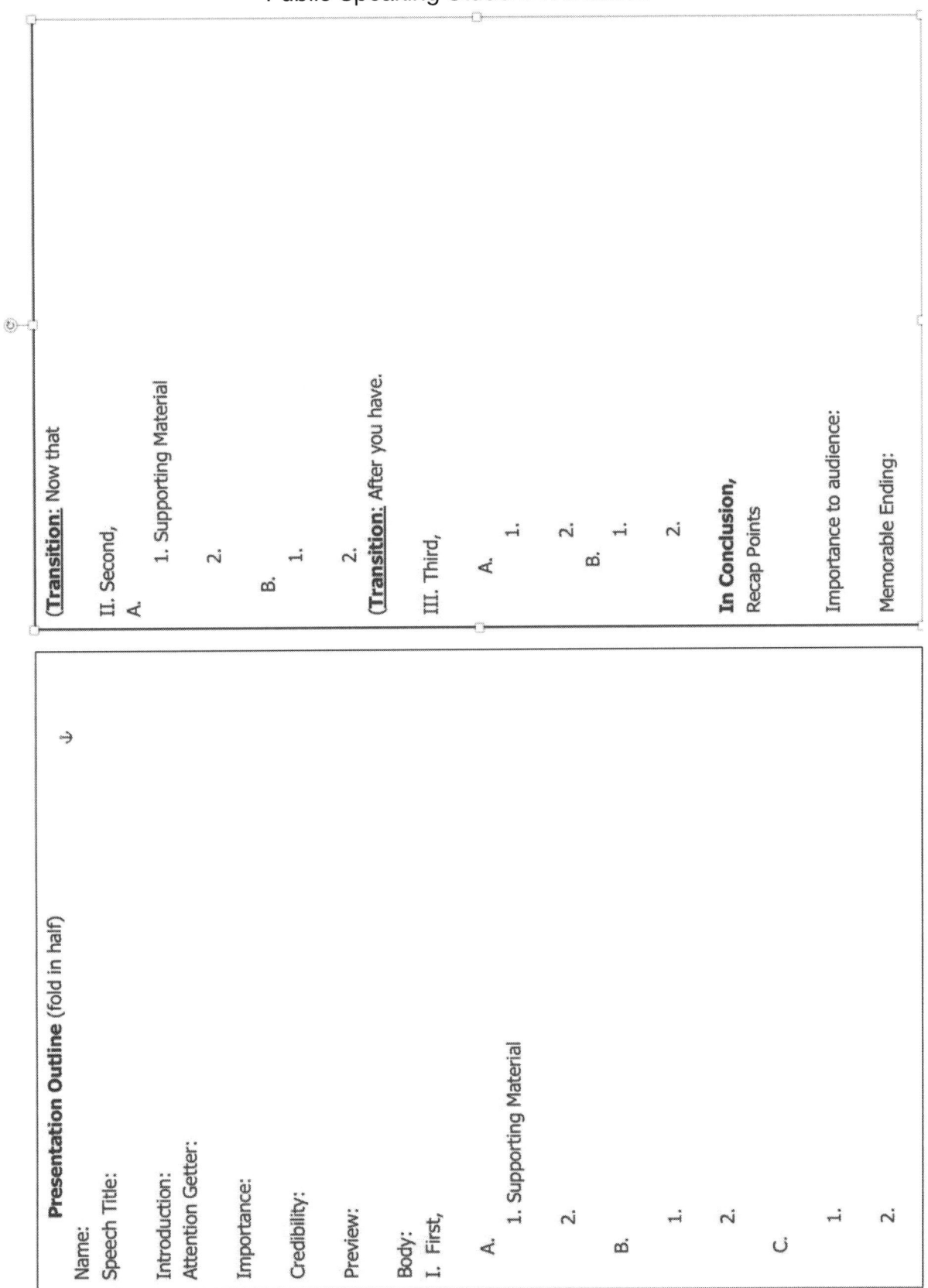

# Appendix

Public Speaking Student Workbook

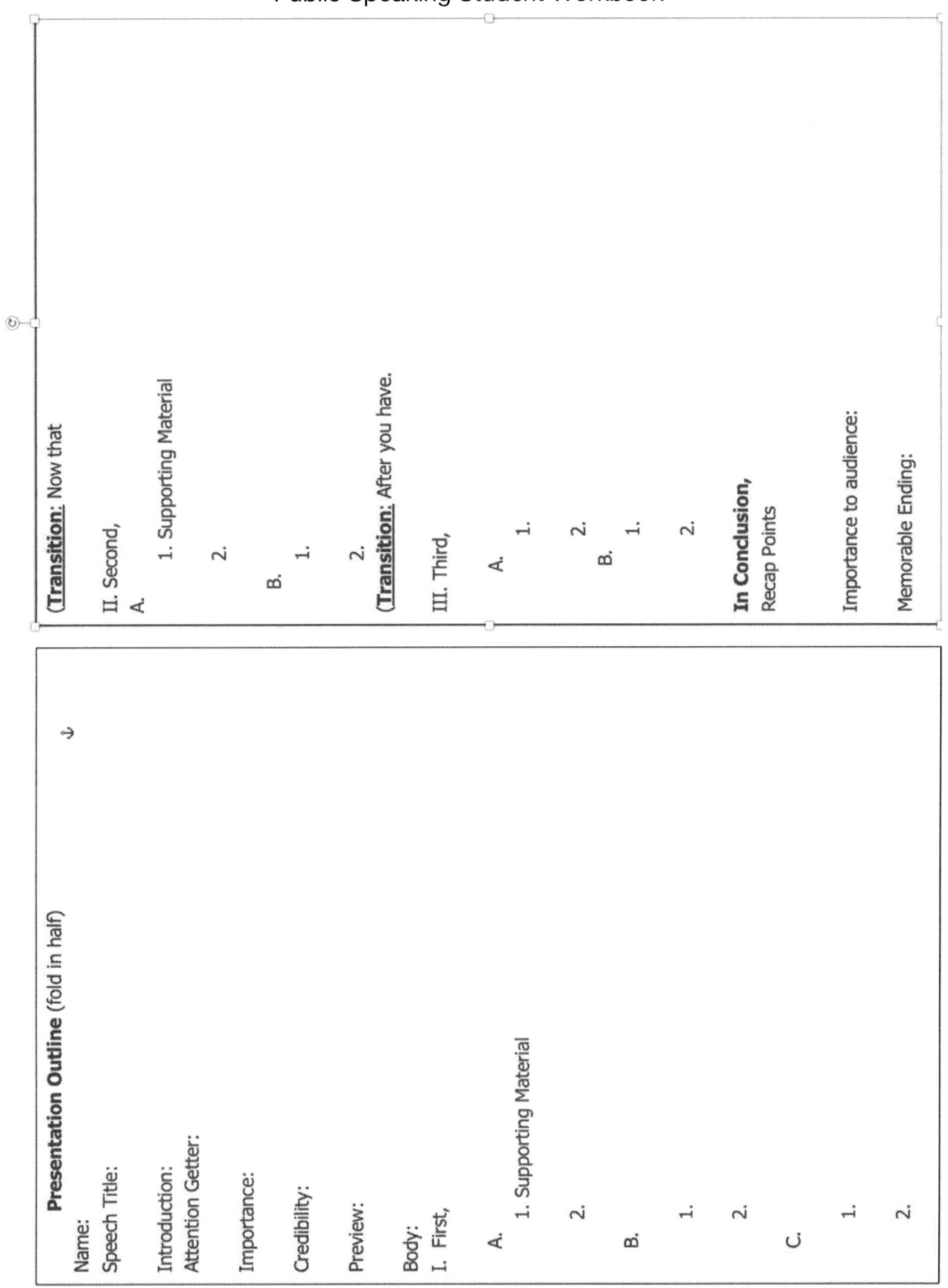

**Presentation Outline** (fold in half)

Name:
Speech Title:

Introduction:
Attention Getter:

Importance:

Credibility:

Preview:

Body:
I. First,
   A.
      1. Supporting Material
      2.
   B.
      1.
      2.
   C.
      1.
      2.

(**Transition**): Now that

II. Second,
   A.
      1. Supporting Material
      2.
   B.
      1.
      2.

(**Transition**): After you have.

III. Third,
   A.
      1.
      2.
   B.
      1.
      2.

**In Conclusion,**
Recap Points

Importance to audience:

Memorable Ending:

247

# Appendix

Made in the USA
Monee, IL
25 February 2025